Editorial Project Manager
Lorin E. Klistoff, M.A.

Editor-in-Chief
Sharon Coan, M.S. Ed.

Illustrators
Howard Chaney
Renée Christine Yates

Cover Artist
Brenda DiAntonis

Art Manager
Kevin Barnes

Art Director
CJae Froshay

Imaging
James Edward Grace
Rosa C. See

Product Manager
Phil Garcia

Publisher
Mary D. Smith, M.S. Ed.

BIBLE
Puzzles and Games

Author

Mary Tucker

D1415796

Teacher Created Resources, Inc.
6421 Industry Way
Westminster, CA 92683
www.teachercreated.com

ISBN: 978-0-7439-7047-1

©*2004 Teacher Created Resources, Inc.*
Reprinted, 2010
Made in U.S.A.

Table of Contents

Table of Contents

Table of Contents

The Bible is God's inspired Word filled with interesting and exciting stories about how God worked through the lives of ordinary people to do extraordinary thngs. Yet, we sometimes present the Bible to children in such a way as to take out all the excitement and adventure. The worst thing we could ever do to our children is make them bored with the Bible! Instead, we should be helping them to see that it is like no other book. It is filled with true stories—people walking across a sea, Jesus walking on a lake, one man being swallowed by a huge fish, a man spending the night with a den of lions, a queen risking her life to save her people, and a teenager giving birth to the Savior of the world in a stable. The best way to help children develop enthusiasm for the Bible is to let them discover its wonders for themselves.

The puzzles and games in this book require children to dig into God's Word to discover God's truths for themselves. They will find out that the Bible stories they read contain truths and lessons that will help them live for God today. Various kinds of puzzles and games are provided to engage the interest of children with all kinds of skills and learning styles. They include the following: crossword puzzles, word searches, coded messages, number/letter blocks, math problem codes, acrostics, scrambled words, putting events in sequence, mazes, hidden messages, count-around puzzles, cross-out word boxes, and much more. Bible references are provided so children can look up answers when they need help or check their work when they are finished. (*Note:* The New International Version is used.) An answer key is provided at the back of the book.

Though it would be impossible to cover the whole Bible in one activity book, the major stories of the Bible are included from Genesis to Revelation. Children will discover how God worked in the lives of Adam and Eve, Noah, Abraham, Sarah, Isaac, Jacob and Rachel, Joseph, Moses, Balaam, Joshua, Rahab, Deborah, Gideon, Samson, Ruth, Hannah, Samuel, Saul, David, Solomon, Elijah and Elisha, Joash, Hezekiah, Nehemiah, Isaiah, Daniel, Jonah, John the Baptist, Peter, Zacchaeus, the early church, Stephen, Philip, Paul, John, and many more, including several stories of Jesus.

As you lead your children through these puzzles and games, be sure to discuss the stories. Ask them to consider what God wants to teach them through each one. Have them share what the story means to them personally and how it helps them know God better and want to serve Him. As they work on the New Testament puzzles and games, children will learn how Jesus came to the earth to die for their sins. Make sure each of your children understands the plan of salvation. Provide opportunities for them to act on what they have learned by asking Jesus into their lives. God did not plan for His Word to be written down just to entertain us with exciting stories or teach us moral lessons. Jesus' disciple John explained the reason for the Bible in one of the books he wrote: "But these are written that you may believe that Jesus is the Christ, the Son of God, and that by believing, you may have life in his name." (John 20:31) That is true not just of the New Testament, but of the whole Bible. Even the Old Testament points us to Jesus, the Savior God promised. Make sure your children understand that God Himself is speaking to them through the Bible. Once they realize that, and dig into it for themselves, they will never be bored with the Bible!

God's Wonderful Creation

(Genesis 1)

Directions: Complete the crossword puzzle with the names of what God created on each of the six days.

Day 1: 5–Down and 13–Across

Day 2: 3–Down

Day 3: 2–Down, 7–Down, 1–Across, and 9–Across

Day 4: 4–Down, 8–Down, and 12–Down

Day 5: 10–Down and 11–Across

Day 6: 4–Across and 6–Across

Adam and Eve's Sin

(Genesis 3)

Directions: The serpent tempted Eve in the Garden of Eden, and Eve gave in and disobeyed God. To find out what she did and why she did it, starting with the word at the arrow, print every third word in order on the lines. Keep going around the word rectangle until you have used all the words. Read the rest of the verse to find out what Adam did after Eve sinned. Print those words on the lines at the bottom of the page. Look up Genesis 3:6 to check your answers.

↓

When	desirable	good	the	for	for	woman	gaining	food	saw	wisdom
was										and
also										that
it										she
tree										pleasing
and	ate	the	eye	and	of	the	some	fruit	to	took	the

Then what did Adam do?

___ ___ ___   ___ ___ ___   ___ ___ ___

___ ___ ___   ___ ___   ___ ___ ___

___ ___ ___ ___ ___ ,   ___ ___   ___ ___ ___

___ ___ ___ ___ ,   ___ ___

___ ___ ___ ___ .

The Great Flood

(Genesis 6-8)

Directions: Find your way through the numbers maze by drawing a line through the numbers that answer the questions. All the numbers will be connected. Start at the arrow. Look up the Bible verses if you need help.

1. How old was Noah when the flood began? (Genesis 7:6)

2. How many days and nights did God say it would rain? (Genesis 7:4)

3. How many days did the waters flood the earth? (Genesis 7:24)

4. How many of each kind of animal did God tell Noah to take on the ark? (Genesis 6:19)

5. When the waters went down enough to uncover the mountaintops, how long did Noah wait before he sent out a raven from the ark? (Genesis 8:6–7)

6. How many days did Noah wait to send the dove out of the ark the second time? (Genesis 8:10)

7. How many days did Noah wait to send the dove out of the ark the third time? (Genesis 8:12)

8. How many people were saved from the flood on Noah's ark? (Genesis 7:13)

6	0	0	3	7	1	7	3
6	7	9	4	4	6	4	9
5	8	2	0	1	5	6	2
3	9	5	4	3	0	3	5
8	7	2	1	6	2	9	4
1	1	9	1	4	3	1	7
5	4	2	7	0	4	5	8
4	1	7	6	9	3	0	2
1	2	3	8	7	9	8	5

Two of Every Animal

(Genesis 6)

Directions: God warned Noah that He was going to flood the earth. Noah was to build a huge boat to save his family and two of every animal. Noah filled the ark with every kind of animal. Find and circle the 20 animals in the word search puzzle. Each animal appears twice.

YAK	BEAR	DOVE	GIRAFFE	LION
MONKEY	RAT	SLOTH	CAMEL	PARROT
TIGER	KANGAROO	RABBIT	COBRA	OSTRICH
DOG	ELEPHANT	RHINO	DEER	FOX

```
O  S  D  M  N  R  A  B  B  I  T  G  Y  A  K
S  L  C  O  B  R  A  E  E  V  L  I  O  N  E
T  O  O  N  V  R  A  T  B  E  A  R  A  I  F
R  T  S  K  W  E  E  L  E  P  H  A  N  T  O
I  H  T  E  L  C  A  M  E  L  L  F  D  X  X
C  E  R  Y  D  P  A  R  R  O  T  F  E  D  C
H  L  I  K  A  N  G  A  R  O  O  E  E  O  O
T  E  C  R  T  I  G  E  R  O  P  Y  R  V  B
L  P  H  L  C  I  R  G  I  R  A  F  F  E  R
C  H  K  A  N  G  A  R  O  O  R  F  V  L  A
A  A  N  Y  G  C  B  H  S  R  R  E  O  A  T
M  N  U  R  A  T  B  I  L  I  O  N  R  X  B
E  T  S  A  S  K  I  N  O  H  T  E  D  A  E
L  R  H  I  N  O  T  O  T  V  E  D  O  G  A
M  O  N  K  E  Y  N  O  H  D  T  I  G  E  R
```

The Tower of Babel

(Genesis 11:1–9)

Directions: Sometimes people's pride makes them go against what they know God wants. That is what the Tower of Babel was all about. Solve the acrostic by using the words that are missing from the sentences below. You will discover why the Tower of Babel was built and what God did about it. Look up the Bible verses if you need help.

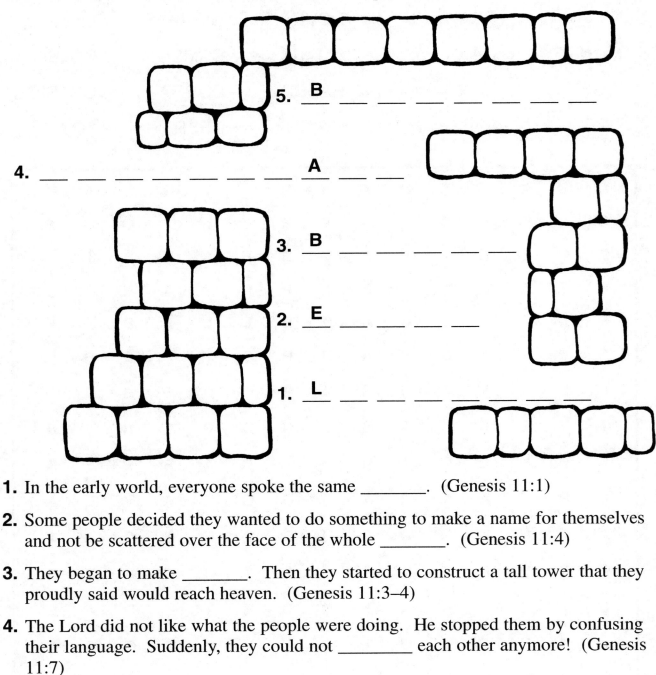

5. B __ __ __ __ __ __ __

4. __ __ __ __ __ __ __ A __ __ __ __

3. B __ __ __ __ __

2. E __ __ __ __ __

1. L __ __ __ __ __ __ __ __

1. In the early world, everyone spoke the same _____. (Genesis 11:1)

2. Some people decided they wanted to do something to make a name for themselves and not be scattered over the face of the whole _____. (Genesis 11:4)

3. They began to make _____. Then they started to construct a tall tower that they proudly said would reach heaven. (Genesis 11:3–4)

4. The Lord did not like what the people were doing. He stopped them by confusing their language. Suddenly, they could not _____ each other anymore! (Genesis 11:7)

5. Then God scattered the people around and the _____ stopped. (Genesis 11:8)

Abraham, Sarah, and Isaac

(Genesis 18:1-15; 21:1-7)

God promised to bless Abraham and build a great nation from him. But 25 years later, he still did not have the son God had promised him! Then God sent three visitors, probably angels, to renew His promise to Abraham. He welcomed them and had them sit down while he brought them food. Sarah stayed in the tent. After they ate, they gave Abraham a message from God.

Directions: Follow the directions to discover what they said and how Sarah responded. Look up Genesis 18:10, 12 to check your work. Cross out all words that are animals, numbers, and colors.

I	will	cat	blue	surely	two	return	purple
to	one	you	about	red	this	time	dog
next	year	four	and	Sarah	pink	your	wife
will	ten	have	a	yellow	lion	son	seven
Sarah	three	laughed	five	to	bear	black	herself

A year later the baby was born. They named him Isaac, which means "he laughs." To find out how old Abraham was when Isaac was born, multiply the number of chapters in the book of Genesis by 2. To find out Sarah's age when she gave birth to Isaac, subtract 10 from Abraham's age. Look up Genesis 21:5 to check your answers.

Abraham was _____ years old.   Sarah was _____ years old.

A Wife for Isaac

(Genesis 24)

Directions: To find out how Isaac got a wife, use the number-letter code. The first word is done for you to show how the code box is to be used. Look up the Bible verses to check your answers.

1	A	B	C	D	E
2	G	H	I	K	L
3	M	N	O	P	R
4	S	T	V	W	Y
	5	6	7	8	9

1. Abraham wanted to find a good wife for Isaac. He sent his <u>S E R V A N T</u>
   4-5 1-9 3-9 4-7 1-5 3-6 4-6

   to his homeland to find just the right woman, hopefully a distant relative. (Genesis 24:10)

2. Abraham promised his servant that _____ would lead him to the right person.
   2-5 3-7 1-8

   (Genesis 24:7)

3. He did not want to make a mistake, so the servant _____. He asked
   3-8 3-9 1-5 4-9 1-9 1-8

   God to bring a woman that would not only give him a drink, but would also water his camels.

   That would be a sign that this was the woman God had chosen for Isaac. (Genesis 24:12–14)

4. A beautiful girl came over. The servant asked her for a drink. She gave it to him, then began to

   pour water for his ten _____! (Genesis 24:19)
   1-7 1-5 3-5 1-9 2-9 4-5

5. As they talked, the servant discovered the girl's family was related to Abraham. He bowed and

   _____ God for answering his prayer. (Genesis 24:26)
   4-8 3-7 3-9 4-5 2-6 2-7 3-8 1-9 1-8

6. The girl whose name was _____ went with Abraham's servant.
   3-9 1-9 1-6 1-9 2-8 1-5 2-6

   When Isaac met her, he loved her and she became his wife. (Genesis 24:67)

Rebekah and Isaac's Twins

(Genesis 25:19–34)

Directions: Rebekah and Isaac had twin boys who grew up to be very different. Solve the math problems to decode the description of the twins. Some letters are given to help you. Look up Genesis 25:27 to check your answers.

A	B	C	D	E	F	G	H	I	J	K	L	M
1	2	3	4	5	6	7	8	9	10	11	12	13
N	O	P	Q	R	S	T	U	V	W	X	Y	Z
14	15	16	17	18	19	20	21	22	23	24	25	26

___ ___ ___ ___   ___ ___ ___ ___ ___ ___   ___ ___
2+3 14+5 7–6 11+10 13–11 20–15 2+1 14–13 7+6 4+1   26–25

___ ___ ___ ___ ___ ___ ___
11+8 5+6 20–11 6+6 10+2 4+2 18+3 19–7

___ ___ ___ ___ ___ ___, ___ ___ ___ ___ ___ ___
4+4 5+16 24–10 10+10 8–3 12+6   3–2 5+8 18–17 20–6 8+7 9–3

___ ___ ___ ___ ___ ___ ___
3+17 13–5 3+2 17–2 8+8 22–17 6+8

___ ___ ___ ___ ___ ___ ___, ___ ___ ___ ___ ___
15–12 9+6 19+2 20–6 18+2 24–6 30–5   20+3 17–9 2+7 8+4 7–2

___ ___ ___ ___ ___ ___ ___ ___ ___
3+7 7–6 16–13 11+4 5–3 26–3 18–17 9+10 14–13

___ ___ ___ ___ ___ ___ ___ ___,
13+4 9+12 15–6 1+4 13+7 10+3 12–11 17–3

___ ___ ___ ___ ___ ___ ___ ___ ___ ___ ___ ___
21–2 6+14 18–17 12+13 13–4 7+7 17–10 23–22 4+9 21–6 26–12 3+4

___ ___ ___ ___ ___ ___ ___ ___.
28–8 19–11 12–7 14+6 11–6 12+2 23–3 12+7

Jacob Works for a Wife

(Genesis 29:1-28)

Directions: Jacob left home and went to live with his Uncle Laban. Unscramble the words and write them in the sentences to complete the story.

---

1. H E A L	2. A C R E H L	3. S V N E E
4. M G R A R I E A	5. E N E V S	6. S E V I W	7. C H R A L E
8. W L T V E E	9. O E P J H S	10. J A M I N N E B

Laban had two daughters. The older girl was named _____.

1

While Jacob was working for Laban, he fell in love with the younger girl,

_____. Jacob promised to work for no pay for _____

2   3

years if Laban would let him marry her. Laban agreed, but when the time was up, he

tricked Jacob and gave him the older daughter instead! When Jacob angrily accused

Laban of deceiving him, Laban said, "We never give a younger daughter in

_____ before the older one." He promised to give Jacob the

4

daughter he wanted if he would agree to work for free for another _____

5

years. Jacob loved her so much, he agreed. So Jacob ended up with two

_____, but the only one he truly loved was _____.

6   7

Many years later, Jacob had _____ sons, but his

8

favorites were always _____ and _____,

9   10

the sons he had with Rachel.

Joseph and His Jealous Brothers

(Genesis 37)

Directions: To find out about Joseph and his jealous brothers, complete the sentences by using letters from the box. Beginning at the arrow, print every other letter in order on the lines in the sentences. When you get to the end of a line of letters, go back to the beginning of the next line in the box. When you get to the bottom of the box, go back to the top line and keep going until you use all the letters.

→ B	I	A	S	D	T	R	E	E	R	P	N	O
S	R	O	T	L	L	D	O	E	V	G	E	Y
D	P	D	T	R	G	E	O	A	A	M	T	S
B	K	L	I	O	L	O	L	D	S	F	T	A
R	T	I	H	P	E	P	R	E	A	D	N	R
I	O	M	B	A	E	L	C					

Why Joseph's older brothers hated him:

1. Joseph gave his father a ___ ___ ___ ___ ___ ___ ___ ___ ___ about them. (He tattled!)

2. Their father ___ ___ ___ ___ ___ Joseph more.

3. Joseph had two ___ ___ ___ ___ ___ ___ that his brothers bowed down to him.

What Joseph's brothers did when he went where they were taking care of the family sheep:

4. They plotted to ___ ___ ___ ___ him.

5. They ___ ___ ___ ___ ___ ___ ___ ___ off Joseph's ___ ___ ___ ___.

6. They threw him into an empty ___ ___ ___ ___ ___ ___ ___.

7. They ___ ___ ___ ___ him to some merchants on their way to ___ ___ ___ ___ ___.

How the brothers covered up their evil act:

8. They killed a ___ ___ ___ ___ and dipped Joseph's robe in its ___ ___ ___ ___ ___.

9. They showed the robe to their ___ ___ ___ ___ ___ ___ and said, "We found this. Is it Joseph's?"

10. Jacob recognized the robe and thought, as his sons hoped he would, that an ___ ___ ___ ___ ___ ___ had killed Joseph.

Joseph in Egypt

(Genesis 37:36; 39–41)

Directions: Joseph's brothers sold him into slavery, and he was taken far away to the land of Egypt. Living and working among idol-worshipers, Joseph trusted God in spite of many troubles. Decode the Bible verse to find out how God rewarded Joseph for his faithfulness. Look up Genesis 39:23 to check your work.

A	C	D	E	G	H	I	J	L	M
➳	●	◆	↕	☽	☛	✉	➤	✞	✳
N	**O**	**P**	**R**	**S**	**T**	**U**	**V**	**W**	
✖	☆	✚	❙	■	▲	★	♣	⊃	

___ ___ ___   ___ ___ ___ ___   ___ ___ ___
▲ ☛ ↕   ✞ ☆ ❙ ◆   ⊃ ➳ ■

___ ___ ___ ___   ___ ___ ___ ___ ___ ___
⊃ ✉ ▲ ☛   ➤ ☆ ■ ↕ ✚ ☛

___ ___ ___   ___ ___ ___ ___   ___ ___ ___
➳ ✖ ◆   ☽ ➳ ♣ ↕   ☛ ✉ ✳

___ ___ ___ ___ ___ ___ ___   ___ ___
■ ★ ● ● ↕ ■ ■   ✉ ✖

___ ___ ___ ___ ___ ___ ___ ___   ___ ___   ___ ___ ___
⊃ ☛ ➳ ▲ ↕ ♣ ↕ ❙   ☛ ↕   ◆ ✉ ◆

Baby in a Basket

(Exodus 2:1-10)

Directions: Do you know the story of baby Moses? Which picture below shows what happened first? Put a number 1 in the box below that picture. Then number the other pictures to show in what order they happened. If you need help, read the whole story in Exodus 2:1–10.

☐ The baby's mother put him in a basket and put it in the river.

☐ The baby's sister brought his mother to nurse him for the Princess until he was older.

☐ The Princess took Moses to raise him as her son in the palace.

☐ One Hebrew family hid their newborn son for three months.

☐ Pharaoh ordered all Hebrew baby boys to be drowned in the river!

☐ Pharaoh's daughter, the Princess, found the Hebrew baby and adopted him as her own.

(Exodus 3)

God had a special message for Moses. He got Moses' attention with a bush that was on fire but never burned up. To discover what God wanted Moses to do, use the numbered letters in the boxes to complete the Bible verse. Put every #1 letter on the #1 lines in order. Do the same with the other numbered letters. When you are finished, look up Exodus 3:10 to check your work.

1 G	2 T	3 M	4 O	1 O	3 Y	4 U	☆
2 O	4 T	1 I	2 P	3 P	1 A	3 E	2 H
1 M	3 O	4 O	4 F	2 A	4 E	1 S	3 P
2 R	4 G	1 E	3 L	1 N	3 E	2 A	1 D
3 T	1 I	1 N	2 O	4 Y	1 G	3 H	2 H
1 Y	3 E	2 T	4 P	1 O	3 I	2 O	3 S
3 R	2 B	4 T	3 A	2 R	3 E	3 L	2 I
2 N	3 I	1 U	3 T	3 E	3 S	2 G	☆

1. __ __. __ __ __ __ __ __ __ __ __ __ __ __

2. __ __ __ __ __ __ __ __ __ __ __ __ __ __ __ __

3. __ __ __ __ __ __ __ __, __ __ __ __

__ __ __ __ __ __ __ __ __ __ __,

4. __ __ __ __ __ __ __ __ __ __ __.

The Ten Plagues

(Exodus 7–12)

Directions: To convince hard-hearted Pharaoh to let God's people leave Egypt, God struck the land with ten plagues, one after the other. Can you name all ten in order? Use the clues to figure them out. Look up the Bible verses to check your answers.

1. River turned to _____

   (**CLUE:** the red liquid in our bodies—Exodus 7:20)

2. _____

   (**CLUE:** Ribbit, Ribbit! Croak!—Exodus 8:6)

3. _____

   (**CLUE:** very tiny insects that bite—Exodus 8:17)

4. _____

   (**CLUE:** dirty, annoying, flying insects with huge eyes—Exodus 8:24)

5. _____ of livestock

   (**CLUE:** opposite of life—Exodus 9:6)

6. _____

   (**CLUE:** painful, reddish bumps on a person or animal's body—Exodus 9:10)

7. _____

   (**CLUE:** lumps of ice, small or large—Exodus 9:23)

8. _____

   (**CLUE:** large insects that are like grasshoppers and eat green plants—
   Exodus 10:13)

9. _____

   (**CLUE:** night with no moon or stars—Exodus 10:22)

10. _____ of firstborn sons

    (**CLUE:** what occurs when you stop breathing and your heart stops—
    Exodus 12:29–30)

Escape from Egypt

(Exodus 12:31-51; 14)

Directions: After God struck Egypt with ten horrible plagues, Pharaoh finally told Moses his people could leave. They hurried away with the help and encouragement of many of the Egyptian people. Help the people find their way through the maze out of Egypt.

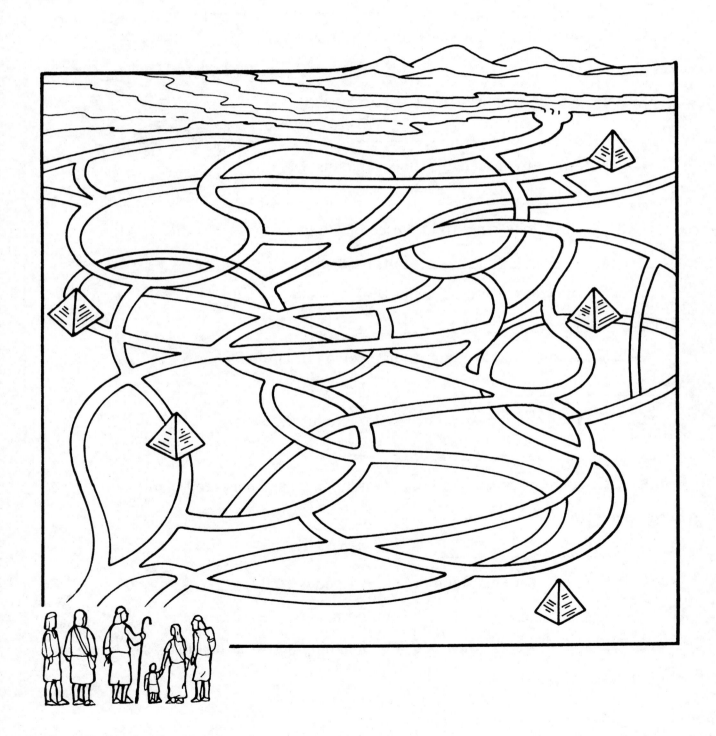

Food and Water for God's People

(Exodus 15:22–17:7)

Directions: After they left Egypt, Moses and his people had a long, hard trip ahead of them. To find out how God provided for them play the game below. Use a small square of paper for a marker. Flip a coin to decide how to move: heads–2 spaces, tails–1 space. When you land on a space, do what it says.

GO BACK 1 SPACE	What did God provide for meat? Exodus 16:13 Go ahead 2 spaces	What is your favorite meat?	What else did God give for food? Exodus 16:14–15	What did the people call the bread? Exodus 16:31 Go ahead 1 space
Why did the people grumble? Exodus 16:1–3 Go ahead 2 spaces				How often were the people to gather the food? Exodus 16:26 Go ahead 1 space
Stay put while you think about God's goodness.				How long did God provide the food? Exodus 16:35 Go ahead 2 spaces
Tell something God has done for you. Go ahead 1 space		GOD PROVIDES ALL OUR NEEDS! **THE END** Thank God for His goodness.		Why did the people complain again? Exodus 17:1–3 Go ahead 2 spaces
How did God provide water to drink? Exodus 15:25 Go ahead 1 space				**GO BACK 1 SPACE**
GO BACK 1 SPACE	Why did the people grumble? Exodus 15:22–24 Go ahead 1 space	**START** ←	↑ Read Psalm 107:8-9.	How did God provide water? Exodus 17:5-6

The Ten Commandments

(Exodus 20)

Directions: Read God's Ten Commandments on this page and think about them. Then decide in which category each one belongs. Color each tablet yellow or blue:

Yellow: Your relationship with God   **Blue:** Your relationship with other people

1
Have no other gods before Me.
(Exodus 20:3)

8
Do not steal.
(Exodus 20:15)

5
Honor your father and mother.
(Exodus 20:12)

4
Keep the Sabbath Day holy.
(Exodus 20:8)

7
Do not commit adultery.
(Exodus 20:14)

2
Do not make idols to bow down to.
(Exodus 20:4)

3
Do not misuse God's name.
(Exodus 20:7)

9
Do not give false testimony.
(Exodus 20:16)

10
Do not covet what belongs to others.
(Exodus 20:17)

6
Do not murder.
(Exodus 20:13)

God's Tabernacle

(Exodus 25-27)

Many years before Solomon built a temple for God in Jerusalem, there was the tabernacle. It was made so Moses and the people could take it apart and carry it with them when they left a place; then set it up in their next location. They took it with them wherever they went. And it was God's idea!

Directions: To complete what God told Moses to do, follow the directions for each word of the verse. Write the words on the numbered lines. Look up Exodus 25:8 to check your work.

---

1. Opposite of "now"
2. Replace the "s" in "save" with an "h."
3. Add an "m" at the end of "the."
4. Replace the "c" in "cake" with an "m."
5. Remove the "n" from "an."
6. The room in a church where people worship
7. Remove the "u" from "four."

8. Opposite of "you"
9. Remove the "h" from "hand."
10. One-letter word for "me"
11. Opposite of "won't"
12. Add a "d" to the front of "well."
13. Add "ong" to the end of "am."
14. Same word as number 3

____ ____ ____ ____   ____ ____   ____ ____ ____
　　　1　　　　　　　　**2**　　　　　　　**3**

____ ____ ____ ____   ____ ____
　　4　　　　　　**5**

____ ____ ____ ____ ____ ____   ____ ____ ____ ____   ____ ____
　　　　　6　　　　　　　　　　　　　　　**7**

____ ____ ,   ____ ____ ____   ____ ____   ____ ____ ____
　8　　　　　**9**　　　　**10**　　　　**11**

____ ____ ____ ____   ____ ____ ____ ____ ____
　　12　　　　　　　　**13**

____ ____ ____ ____ .
　　14

Who designed the tabernacle? Read Exodus 25:9 to find out!

Offerings for the Lord

(Leviticus 1-5)

Directions: In Old Testament days God's people worshiped God with special offerings. They brought them to the priests to sacrifice. Read about some of them below. Then cross out the letters that spell the word WORSHIP, working left to right, in each box. The letters that are left will spell the names of the offerings. Write the names of the offerings on the lines.

1. To worship God and ask for forgiveness of unintentional sin, people could offer a bull, a ram, or a male dove or pigeon.

> This was a BWURONT ROSFHFEIRIPNG.
>
> _____ _____

2. To worship God for His goodness and thank Him for providing, people could offer flour or grain, olive oil, bread, or salt.

> This was a GRWAOIRNS HOFFIERPING.
>
> _____ _____

3. To worship and thank God, with a group meal afterwards, people could offer any animal from their herds or flocks or they could offer bread.

> This was a FWELLOOWSHRIP SOHFIFEPRING.
>
> _____ _____

4. Because everyone sins, sometimes without meaning to, all the people had to make this offering of a young bull, a goat, a dove or pigeon, or some flour. What you offered depended on how much money you had and how important your place was in the community.

> This was a WSOIRNS OFHFEIRINPG.
>
> _____ _____

5. To ask for forgiveness from unintentional sin which caused damage or loss, the people had to offer a ram or a lamb and pay a fine.

> This was a WGOUIRLST OHFFERIINPG.
>
> _____ _____

Clean and Unclean Foods

(Leviticus 11)

Directions: When God gave His people the Ten Commandments, He also gave them some important rules about eating. He told them they could eat the meat of any animal that had split hooves and chewed a cud. The people could eat any water creatures that had fins and scales, but nothing else. The book of Leviticus lists some of these animals, as well as some birds the people were forbidden to eat. Read each clue; then choose the creature it describes. Write the name of the creature on the line. Use the guidelines God gave to figure out other creatures God's people could or could not eat.

_____ 1. I hop on big feet, but God says, "Don't eat!"

_____ 2. I'm fat and I squeal, but I'm not for your meal.

_____ 3. My fins and scales swish as I swim. Just your dish!

_____ 4. I moo as I chew my cud. I'm for you!

_____ 5. I come flying at night. Don't you dare take a bite!

_____ 6. I crawl on all fours, but I'm no meal of yours!

_____ 7. I'm a bug; yes it's true, but I'm still food for you.

_____ 8. "Hoo! Hoo!" I say. But don't eat me; no way!

_____ 9. I live in a shell in the sea. Don't eat me!

_____ 10. "Baa! Baa!" I say. Eating me is okay.

owl   clam   rabbit   lizard   pig

sheep   grasshopper   trout   bat   cow

The Twelve Tribes of Israel

(Genesis 49; Numbers 1)

Directions: Find and circle the 12 tribes of Israel in the word search puzzle. Write the leftover letters in order on the lines below to find out where the twelve tribes of Israel began and from whom they got their names.

REUBEN

SIMEON

LEVI

JUDAH

ZEBULUN

ISSACHAR

DAN

GAD

ASHER

NAPHTALI

JOSEPH

BENJAMIN

G	D	J	L	E	V	I	B
A	A	S	H	E	R	N	E
Z	N	D	C	R	O	A	N
E	O	B	S	E	T	P	J
B	W	E	M	U	J	H	A
U	J	I	L	B	O	T	M
L	S	U	V	E	S	A	I
U	E	S	D	N	E	L	N
N	O	N	S	A	P	I	*
I	S	S	A	C	H	A	R

___ ___ ___ ___ ___ , ___

___ ___ ___ ___ ___ ___ ___ ___ ___

Exploring Canaan

(Numbers 13–14)

Directions: Before the Israelites went into Canaan, the land God had promised them, Moses sent 12 men, one from each tribe, to explore the land. Read the questions Moses wanted answered. This is your code. Use the numbered letters to decode what Joshua and Caleb, two godly spies, believed after they saw the land.

```
        ARE THE PEOPLE STRONG OR WEAK?
        1       2  3  4        5           6

  ARE THE TOWNS THEY LIVE IN UNWALLED OR FORTIFIED?
    7       8  9       10       11        12

           IS THE SOIL FERTILE OR POOR?
              13       14      15
```

Joshua and Caleb believed

____ ____   ____ ____ ____   ____ ____ ____ ____
10   14   9   7   2   15   4   5   12

____ ____   ____ ____ ____ ____ ____ ____ ____
10   13   3   15   2   1   13   2   12

____ ____ ____ ____   ____ ____,   ____ ____
 6   10   9   7   11   13   7   2

____ ____ ____ ____   ____ ____ ____ ____   ____ ____
 6   10   15   15   15   2   1   12   11   13

____ ____ ____ ____   ____ ____ ____ ____
10   8   9   4   9   7   1   9

____ ____ ____ ____. (Numbers 14:8)
15   1   8   12

Balaam and His Talking Donkey

(Numbers 22)

Directions: God had to use a talking donkey to get Balaam's attention! Read the story in Numbers 22. Then complete the Bible verses below to find out what happened after the donkey and Balaam had a conversation. Cross out the double letters in the words; then write the remaining letters in order on the lines. Look up Numbers 22:31–33 to check your work.

Then the Lord opened Balaam's eyes, and he saw the _____
(IIAMMNKKGERRL)

of the Lord standing in the road with his _____ drawn. So he
(SXXWUUORPPD)

_____ low and fell face down. The _____
(BRROWGGED)   (AZZNMMGETTL)

of the Lord asked Balaam, "Why have you beaten your donkey these three times?

I have come here to oppose you because your _____ is a
(UUPMMAYYTH)

reckless one before me. The _____ saw me and turned
(BBDOJJNHHKLLEY)

_____ from me these three times. If she had not turned
(AEEWPPAY)

_____, I would certainly have killed _____
(OOAWQQANNY)   (UUYNNOU)

by now, but I would have _____ her."
(SRRPAVVRED)

Read verse 34 to see what Balaam said.

Moses' Last Days

(Deuteronomy 32–34)

Moses was God's chosen leader of the Israelites for more than 40 years. He led the people out of Egypt, through the desert, and to the brink of the Promised Land. But that was as far as he would go. He was an old man, and it was time for someone younger to take over. Joshua was the one chosen to lead the people into the Promised Land. Before he died, Moses spoke to the people and blessed them.

Directions: Look up Deuteronomy 33:29 and add the missing words to the Bible verse below to discover what he said to them. Then fit the words you added into the crossword puzzle.

"_____ are you, O Israel! Who is like you, a
                5

_____ _____ by the _____?
        1   6   7

He is your _____ and _____ and your
                    3   4

glorious _____. Your _____ will cower
                8   2

before you and you will trample down their high places."

(Joshua 1)

Moses was dead, and Joshua was the new leader of God's people. Joshua had been training for this job for years as Moses' aide. Now he was ready to obey the Lord and do whatever he was told. What was the first thing God told Joshua and the people to do? Follow the directions to find out.

Directions: In the word pairs below, one word has a letter that is not in the other word. Write it on the line with the matching number in the box. When you are finished, you will know what Joshua and the people had to do. Look up Joshua 1:2 to check your answer.

1. I'm in CAT but not in RAT.

2. Find me in THROUGH but not in THOUGH.

3. Here I am in FOX but I'm missing from FIX.

4. I'm twice in PASS but not in PAT.

5. I'm present in FOOT but absent from FOOL.

6. You'll see me in BOTH but not in BOAT.

7. I'm in FEAR but not in FAR.

8. You can find me in JUG but not in MUG.

9. I'm found in DOG but not in HOG.

10. I'm in BEGAN but not BEGIN.

11. See me in LONG but not in LOG.

12. You'll find me in MILL but not in MALL.

13. I'm found in VAT but not in FAT.

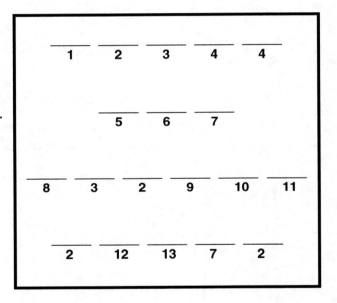

Why did God want Joshua and the people to do this first?

Rahab and the Israelite Spies

(Joshua 2)

Directions: Joshua sent two spies to secretly go over into the Promised Land and check things out, especially the city of Jericho. A kind woman named Rahab hid them on her roof from the king, then let them down the city wall by a rope. Help the two spies find their way home through the maze from Rahab's house below.

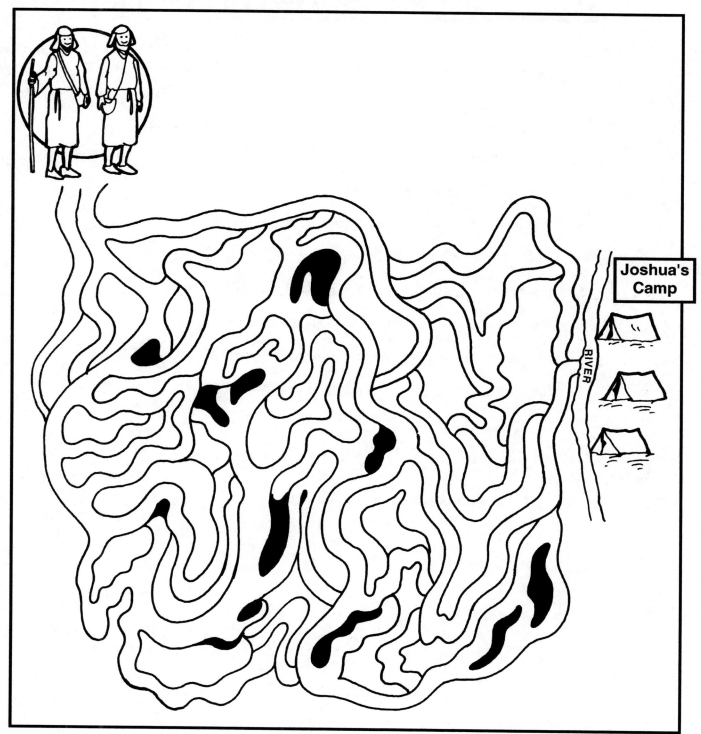

Conquering Jericho

(Joshua 6)

Directions: God told Joshua exactly what to do to conquer the city of Jericho, and Joshua did what He said. Numbers are important in this story. Write the correct number in front of each thing that happened.

| 1 | 2 | 3 | 4 | 5 | 6 | 7 | 8 | 9 | 10 |

_____ **a.** How many times the people marched around Jericho the first day

_____ **b.** How many days they did this

_____ **c.** How many priests carried rams' horn trumpets

_____ **d.** How many days the priests blew their trumpets

_____ **e.** How many times the people marched around Jericho the seventh day

_____ **f.** How many days the people were silent as they marched around the city

_____ **g.** How many days the people shouted as they marched

_____ **h.** How many families in Jericho were not destroyed

_____ **i.** How many men went to bring out Rahab's family

Who knocked down the walls of Jericho? Write the answer on the line below. (*Hint:* The number of letters in the answer is the number that you used most often to answer the questions above.) After you answer, look up Joshua 6:2 again to see if you are right.

_____ _____

Destroying Ai

(Joshua 8)

Directions: The first time Joshua and his army attacked Ai, they were badly defeated. Joshua could not understand why God had not helped them as He did at Jericho. Then he found out that one of his men had sinned by taking some silver and gold from Jericho and hiding it in his tent. Achan was punished. Then God promised to help them conquer Ai. Number the events of that battle to put them in correct order.

Early in the morning Joshua led his army toward Ai.

When Joshua signaled, the soldiers hiding behind Ai ran into the city and set it on fire.

The men of Ai saw that their city was on fire.

During the night, Joshua sent part of his army to wait behind Ai to ambush the city at his signal.

Ai's army hurried out of the city to chase Joshua's army when they saw them coming.

Joshua's men turned around and attacked Ai's army. They were caught in the middle with no way to escape.

The Tricky Gibeonites

(Joshua 9)

The people of Gibeon heard how God had helped the Israelites conquer Jericho and Ai. They were afraid they might be next, so they came up with a plan to trick Joshua. They sent men dressed in ragged clothing with moldy bread to the Israelite camp. Of course, everyone thought the Gibeonites had traveled a great distance. They told Joshua they had come from a faraway land to make a peace treaty with Israel. Joshua and the Israelites were fooled by their neighbors, the Gibeonites, and agreed to a peace treaty.

Directions: To find out why Joshua and the Israelites were so easily fooled, begin at the arrow and print every other letter in order on the lines. When you get to the end of a line of letters, go to the beginning of the next line. Go through the letters twice to complete the verse.

→ T	S	H	I	E	O	M	N	E	S
N	B	O	U	F	T	I	D	S	I
R	D	A	N	E	O	L	T	S	I
A	N	M	Q	P	U	L	I	E	R
D	E	T	O	H	F	E	T	I	H
R	E	P	L	R	O	O	R	V	D
I	★	★	★	★	★	★	★	★	★

___ ___ ___ ___ ___ ___ ___ ___ ___ ___ ___ ___ ___

___ ___ ___ ___ ___ ___ ___ ___

___ ___ ___ ___ ___ ___ ___ ___ ___

___ ___ ___ ___ ___ ___ ___ ___ ___

___ ___ ___ ___ ___ ___ ___ ___ . (Joshua 9:14)

Deborah and Barak

(Judges 4–5)

Directions: The story of Deborah and Barak is a story of a great battle won by the Lord. To find out more about what happened, read the clues, look up the Bible verses, and write the correct words on the crossover lines.

---

1. After _____ died, the Israelites once again did _____ in the eyes of the Lord. (Judges 4:1)

   __ __ __ __

   __

   __

   __

---

2. The Lord had given Israel into the hands of this king. (Judges 4:2)

   __ __ __ __ __

   __

   __

   __

   __

   God chose him to help Deborah. (Judges 4:6)

---

3. The enemy commander with 900 iron chariots in his army (Judges 4:2)

   __ __ __ __ __ __

   __

   __

   __

   __

   Deborah helped lead this army. (Judges 4:6, 9)

   __

---

4. Israelites came to her to judge their disputes. (Judges 4:4–5)

   __ __ __ __ __ __ __

   __

   __

   __

   __

   She held court in the hill country of _____. (Judges 4:4–5)

   __

Gideon's Army

(Judges 6-7)

Directions: Gideon could not believe that God had chosen him to save Israel from the Midianites! There was nothing special about him; he was not brave or even a good leader. But, of course, God planned to use His strength, not Gideon's, to defeat the enemy. The army He had Gideon choose and the unusual way He told Gideon to attack the enemy prove that it was God's will. Decode the words and numbers to complete the facts.

CODE												
A	**B**	**C**	**D**	**E**	**F**	**G**	**H**	**I**	**J**	**K**	**L**	**M**
0	1	2	3	4	5	6	7	8	9	10	11	12
N	**O**	**P**	**Q**	**R**	**S**	**T**	**U**	**V**	**W**	**X**	**Y**	**Z**
13	14	15	16	17	18	19	20	21	22	23	24	25

Gideon's Army

God told Gideon his army was too big! Gideon told them that anyone who was afraid could go home and 22,000 soldiers went home! That left him with _____ men. God said that was
B   A   A   A   A

still too many! Gideon took everyone down to the water for a drink. Most of the men got on their knees to drink. Others scooped the water into their hands and lapped it up, and those were the ones God said should remain in the army. When the others left, Gideon ended up with an army of

_____ soldiers! Now when Israel beat the Midianites, everyone would know that it was
D   A   A

not the strength of the army that did it, but God!

An Unusual Battle

God told Gideon to give all his soldiers _____ and _____
19 17 20 12 15 4 19 18   19 14 17 2 7 4 18

with _____ over them. They sneaked up on the sleeping Midianites one night; then at
9 0 17 18

Gideon's signal, they blew their _____, broke their _____,
19 17 20 12 15 4 19 18   9 0 17 18

and_____, "A sword for the Lord and for Gideon!" Suddenly, the Midianites
18 7 14 20 19 4 3

heard loud noises and saw fire all around them. They panicked and began fighting each other. Gideon

and his soldiers easily defeated them. But it was clear that God was the one who gave them victory.

Strong Samson

(Judges 13–16)

Directions: Samson did not always obey God, but God used him to fight Israel's enemies. Look at the words in the boxes. Cross out the letters that spell STRONG, working left to right, in each box. Write the remaining letters on the lines. Then match each of the words to the correct descripton.

_____ **1.** Told Manoah's wife she was going to have a son. (Judges 13:3)

_____ **2.** What Samson's parents were told he would be. (Judges 13:5)

_____ **3.** The enemies God would fight with using Samson. (Judges 13:5)

_____ **4.** The Spirit of the Lord gave Samson strength to kill this animal when it ran at him. (Judges 14:6)

_____ **5.** Samson struck down 1000 enemy soldiers with the jawbone of this animal. (Judges 15:15)

_____ **6.** Samson fell in love with her, but she betrayed him. (Judges 16:4)

_____ **7.** Samson's enemies wanted to find out the secret of his _____. (Judges 16:5)

_____ **8.** His enemies made Samson weak by shaving off his _____. (Judges 16:19)

_____ **9.** Samson killed thousands of his enemies and himself by pushing down the pillars of their _____. (Judges 16:30)

A STLRIOONNG _____

B DSETLRIOLNAHG _____

C STANRGOENLG _____

D HSTRAOINGR _____

E SPTHIRLISOTINNGES _____

F DSOTRONNKEGY _____

G SSTTRROENNGGTH _____

H NSATROZNIRIGTE _____

I STTEROMNPLGE _____

Faithful Ruth

(Ruth 1–4)

Directions: God blessed Ruth for her faithfulness to her mother-in-law Naomi. Show the order in which the events in Ruth's story happened by drawing a line from the first event to the second, then on to the third, and so on until they are all connected. Then number them from 1 to 7.

A. _____
Ruth's
husband dies.

B. _____
Ruth works
in Boaz's
fields.

C. _____
Ruth gives
birth to a son,
Obed.

D. _____
Ruth meets
Boaz.

E. _____
Ruth marries
Naomi's son.

F. _____
Ruth and
Naomi go to
Bethlehem.

G. _____
Ruth and
Boaz get
married.

When Obed became an old man, who was his famous grandson? _____

Hannah's Baby

(1 Samuel 1)

Directions: Hannah had no children, so she asked the Lord to give her a son. God answered her prayer. To find out how Hannah showed her thankfulness to God, use the number/letter code box to complete what she said to Eli, the priest.

1	A	C	D	E
2	G	H	I	L
3	N	O	P	R
4	S	V	W	Y
	5	6	7	8

Hannah told Eli, " I ___ ___ ___ ___ ___ ___ for this ___ ___ ___ ___ ___ and
               3-7 3-8 1-5 4-8 1-8 1-7   1-6 2-6 2-7 2-8 1-7

the ___ ___ ___ ___ has granted me what I asked of him. So now I ___ ___ ___ ___
    2-8 3-6 3-8 1-7   2-5 2-7 4-6 1-8

him to the ___ ___ ___ ___. For his ___ ___ ___ ___ ___ life he will be
           2-8 3-6 3-8 1-7   4-7 2-6 3-6 2-8 1-8

___ ___ ___ ___ ___ over to the ___ ___ ___ ___." (1 Samuel 1:27–28)
2-5 2-7 4-6 1-8 3-5   2-8 3-6 3-8 1-7

Samuel Serves God

(1 Samuel 3)

Directions: Samuel had an unusual childhood. When he was three years old, his mother took him to live at the Lord's tabernacle at Shiloh. He grew up there, helping Eli, the priest, and learning to serve the Lord. God called Samuel when he was just a boy. To find out what happened in his later life, cross out all the double letters in the letters below. When you get to the end of a line, go to the beginning of the next line. Write the remaining letters in order on the lines.

T	S	S	H	M	M	E	L	O	P	P	R	D	Z	Z	W	I	I	A
S	B	B	W	I	U	U	T	H	S	A	V	V	M	U	C	C	E	L
A	S	F	F	H	W	W	E	G	R	E	A	A	W	U	P	A	Z	Z
N	D	I	S	E	E	R	A	E	K	K	L	R	E	C	G	G	O	G
N	I	P	P	Z	E	D	T	J	J	H	A	Q	Q	T	S	A	O	O
M	U	E	L	W	R	R	A	S	A	P	R	O	Y	Y	P	H	G	G
E	T	O	F	T	H	Y	Y	E	L	C	C	O	J	J	R	B	B	D

__ __ __ __ __ __ __ __ __ __ __ __

__ __ __ __ __ __ __ __ __ __ __ __

__ __ __ __ __ __ __ __ __ __ __ __ ,

... __ __ __ __ __ __ __ __

__ __ __ __ __ __ __ __ __ __

__ __ __ __ __ __ __ __ __ __ __ __

__ __ __ __ __ __ __ __ __ __ __ .

(1 Samuel 3:19–20)

Israel's First King

(1 Samuel 8-10)

Directions: The people of Israel asked for a king. Samuel tried to talk them out of it because God was their ruler. But God said, "Listen to them and give them a king." (1 Samuel 8:22) The man God chose did not know he was going to be king until Samuel anointed him! What was the first king like? To find out, print the letter that comes <u>after</u> each letter given. (*Note:* For the letter "after" Z, use A.) When you are finished, draw a picture of the king.

A	B	C	D	E	F	G	H	I	J	K	L	M
N	O	P	Q	R	S	T	U	V	W	X	Y	Z

God chose ___ ___ ___ ___ , an impressive ___ ___ ___ ___ ___
         R   Z   T   K   X   N   T   M   F

man without ___ ___ ___ ___ ___ among the Israelites—
            D   P   T   Z   K

a ___ ___ ___ ___   ___ ___ ___ ___ ___ ___ than
   G   D   Z   C   S   Z   K   K   D   Q

any of the ___ ___ ___ ___ ___ ___ . (1 Samuel 9:2)
         N   S   G   D   Q   R

ILLUSTRATION

(1 Samuel 14)

Directions: Saul's son Jonathan bravely attacked the Philistines with only his armor bearer. Nobody in Israel's army, including Saul, knew what Jonathan was doing until they saw the Philistines running in panic. Did Jonathan believe he and his armor bearer could defeat the enemy? To find out, write the letters in the number 1 boxes on line 1, the letters in the number 2 boxes on line 2, and so on until you have used all the letters. Work left to right.

N 1	I 6	G 3	H 1	H 6	T 2	O 5	N 4
C 2	I 6	H 4	E 6	D 3	O 6	A 4	N 5
D 6	R 2	M 6	R 3	A 1	E 5	N 1	F 2
T 1	R 5	O 3	✡	I 2	H 4	T 6	L 1
Y 4	G 3	W 2	V 5	E 3	✡	H 5	R 2
N 6	B 3	B 5	S 1	N 1	Y 2	A 4	M 5
E 2	✡	O 6	F 5	R 4	W 3	Y 4	E 1

Jonathan said to his armor bearer, "Come, let's go . . . . Perhaps the Lord will act in our behalf.

___ ___ ___ ___ ___ ___ ___   ___ ___ ___
 1   5   2   1   6   4   3   2   1   5

___ ___ ___ ___ ___ ___   ___ ___ ___   ___ ___ ___ ___
 6   6   1   3   6   2   1   4   5   1   6   3   6

___ ___ ___ ___   ___ ___ ___ ___ ___ ___,
 2   5   3   6   1   4   5   2   1   3

___ ___ ___ ___ ___ ___ ___   ___ ___   ___ ___ ___ ___
 2   5   1   6   4   3   2   5   4   5   4   6   2

                                    " (1 Samuel 14:6)
___ ___   ___ ___   ___ ___ ___.
 6   4   3   4   5   2   3

God Chooses David

(1 Samuel 16:1-13)

Directions: God was not pleased with King Saul, so He told Samuel He was going to choose a new king for Israel. He told Samuel to go to the town of Bethlehem to anoint the king who would be one of Jesse's eight sons. Number the pictures from 1 to 6 to show the order in which they happened when Samuel anointed the king God had chosen.

_____ After seeing seven of Jesse's sons Samuel asked, "Are these all the sons you have?"

_____ Abinadab passed by Samuel, but Samuel said, "The Lord has not chosen him."

_____ Samuel anointed David, Jesse's youngest son, and God's Spirit came upon David.

_____ Samuel saw Eliab, the oldest, and thought he must be the one God had chosen.

_____ God said, "Man looks at the outward appearance, but the Lord looks at the heart."

_____ Jesse sent for David, and God told Samuel, "Rise and anoint him; he is the one."

David and Goliath

(1 Samuel 17)

Directions: David was only a teenager, but he was brave enough to face a giant who was at least three feet taller than he was. Follow the directions to find out more about David and the giant.

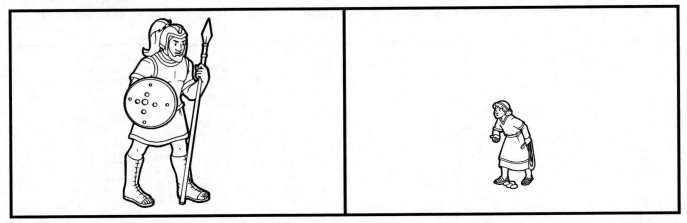

1. Next to David, write what he told King Saul about his strength and courage. (1 Samuel 17:34–35)

2. Next to Goliath, write what King Saul said about him. (1 Samuel 17:33)

3. Choose the weapons from the box below that Goliath had. List them next to him. Then list David's weapons next to him. (1 Samuel 17:4, 40)

bronze helmet	bronze armor	bronze javelin	five stones
bronze leg armor	sling	shield	huge spear

4. Use the following clues to complete the words David said to Goliath about his secret weapon.

A. Another word for "me"

B. Opposite of "go"

C. Add "st" to the end of "again."

D. Opposite of "me"

E. Opposite of "out"

F. What you are called is your _____.

G. Another name for "God"

H. Bible word for "most powerful"

DAVID SAID TO GOLIATH, "YOU COME AGAINST ME WITH SWORD AND SPEAR AND JAVELIN, BUT

___ ___ ___ ___
A   B

___ ___ ___ ___ ___ ___ ___ ___ ___
C

___ ___ ___ ___ ___ THE
D   E

___ ___ ___ OF THE
F

___ ___ ___ ___
G

___ ___ ___ ___ ___ ___ ___ ___."
H

David and Jonathan: Best Friends

(1 Samuel 18:1-4; 20:1-42)

Directions: Use the clues to complete the crossword puzzle about David and Jonathan. **A** words go across; **D** words go down.

CLUES

- Jonathan loved David as much as he loved **3-A**. The Bible says they were one in **4-D**. (1 Samuel 18:1)

- To seal their friendship, Jonathan gave David his own **8-A** and his **7-D**. (1 Samuel 18:4)

- Jonathan and David made a **5-D** (agreement) to always be friends. (1 Samuel 18:3)

- Saul, Jonathan's **1-D,** hated David. (1 Samuel 20:1)

- Jonathan found out that Saul planned to kill David, so Jonathan warned David so David could escape secretly. Jonathan knew David would one day be king, so he asked him to always show **2-D** to him and his **6-D**. (1 Samuel 20:14–15)

- When David went away, Jonathan said to him, "Go in peace, for we have sworn **6-A** with each other in the name of the **9-A**. (1 Samuel 20:42)

Saul and the Witch of Endor

(1 Samuel 28)

Directions: King Saul was facing a battle with the Philistines, and he was scared! He decided to visit a medium, a woman who said she could talk to the spirits of dead people. Why? Samuel was dead, but Saul wanted to call him and ask for his advice. Amazingly, Samuel appeared, but what he had to say to Saul was not good news. Use the phone code to discover what he told King Saul. (Examples: -2 = A, 2 = B, 2- = C)

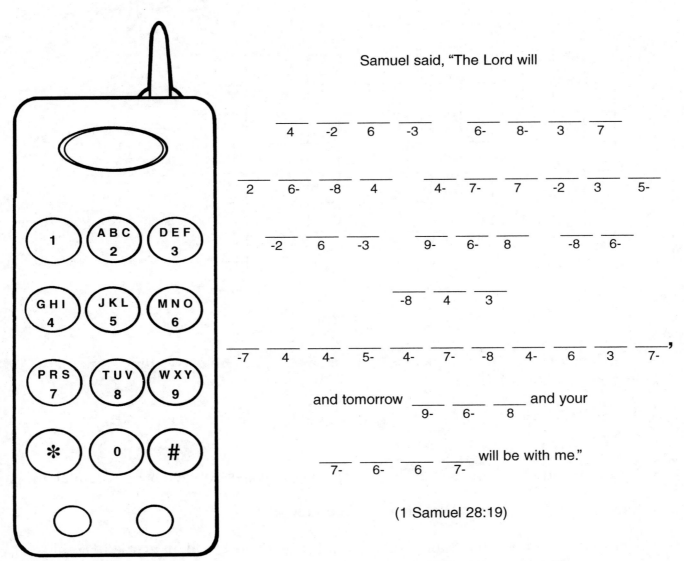

Samuel said, "The Lord will

___ ___ ___ ___   ___ ___ ___ ___
4   -2   6   -3   6-   8-   3   7

___ ___ ___ ___   ___ ___ ___ ___ ___ ___
2   6- -8   4   4-   7-   7   -2   3   5-

___ ___ ___   ___ ___ ___   ___ ___
-2   6   -3   9-   6-   8   -8   6-

___ ___ ___
-8   4   3

___ ___ ___ ___ ___ ___ ___ ___ ___ ___ ___,
-7   4   4-   5-   4-   7-   -8   4-   6   3   7-

and tomorrow ___ ___ ___ and your
              9-   6-   8

___ ___ ___ ___ will be with me."
7-   6-   6   7-

(1 Samuel 28:19)

What do you think Samuel meant?

David Defeats the Philistines

(2 Samuel 5)

Saul was dead and David was the new king of Israel. When Israel's enemies, the Philistines, heard about this, they went full force against him. The huge army spread out across the valley. Wisely, David asked the Lord what he should do. "Go, for I will surely hand the Philistines over to you," God told him. David did what God said and beat the Philistines. But it was not long before they were back after the new king. Once again, David asked the Lord what to do.

Directions: Follow the directions to find out what God told him to do to defeat the Philistines. Use these clues to find some important words.

1. Opposite of "retreat" _____

2. Basic round shape _____

3. Opposite of "slowly" _____

4. Opposite of "crooked" _____

5. Means the same as "hit" _____

6. Walking in rhythm _____

7. Opposite of "back" _____

8. Another name for "God" _____

9. Opposite of "ahead" _____

10. Very tall plants with leaves _____

Directions: Now use those important words to complete the Bible verse. One word is used twice.

God told David, "Do not go _____ up, but _____ around
                                    4   2

_____ them and _____ them in front of the balsam
        9   1

_____. As soon as you hear the sound of _____ in the tops
        10   6

of the balsam _____, move _____, because that will mean
                      10   3

the _____ has gone out in _____ of you to
            8   7

_____ the Philistine army." (2 Samuel 5:23–24)
        5

Read 2 Samuel 5:25 to find out what happened.

King David

(2 Samuel 7-8)

David was a good king who loved God and wanted to build a great temple for Him, but God said no. David's son would be the one to build the temple. However, God gave King David victory over Israel's enemies, the Philistines and the Moabites, and others. And God made a wonderful promise to David.

Directions: Cross out every **C**, **J**, **P**, **Q**, and **X** to discover God's promise. Write the remaining letters in order on the lines below the box.

Y	C	O	U	P	R	H	O	C	U	S	E
A	X	N	C	D	Y	O	J	U	R	K	I
N	X	G	D	C	O	M	W	I	X	L	L
C	E	N	J	D	U	R	C	E	C	F	O
J	R	E	V	P	E	R	B	X	C	E	F
J	O	R	E	M	Q	E	Y	O	X	U	R
T	H	C	R	J	O	N	P	E	W	I	L
L	B	E	E	S	T	C	A	B	L	I	S
H	Q	E	D	F	O	R	C	E	V	E	R

_____ _____ _____ _____ _____ _____

_____ _____ _____ _____ _____ _____

_____ _____ _____ _____ _____ _____

_____ _____ _____ _____ _____ ; _____ _____ _____

_____ _____ _____ _____ _____ _____

_____ _____ _____ _____ _____ _____ _____ . (2 Samuel 7:16)

David and Mephibosheth

(2 Samuel 9)

David and Jonathan were best friends, but then Jonathan and his father Saul were killed in a battle and David became king of Israel. In those days, it was accepted practice for a new king to get rid of all the family members of the king who had come before him. David was a man of God and did not want to harm any of his best friend's relatives. One day King David thought about how he had promised to show kindness to Jonathan's family when he was gone. He sent for Jonathan's crippled son Mephibosheth (Muh-fib-o-sheth).

Directions: Help Mephibosheth find his way to King David. Then write the letters you pass through on the lines below to discover one of the ways David showed Jonathan's son special attention.

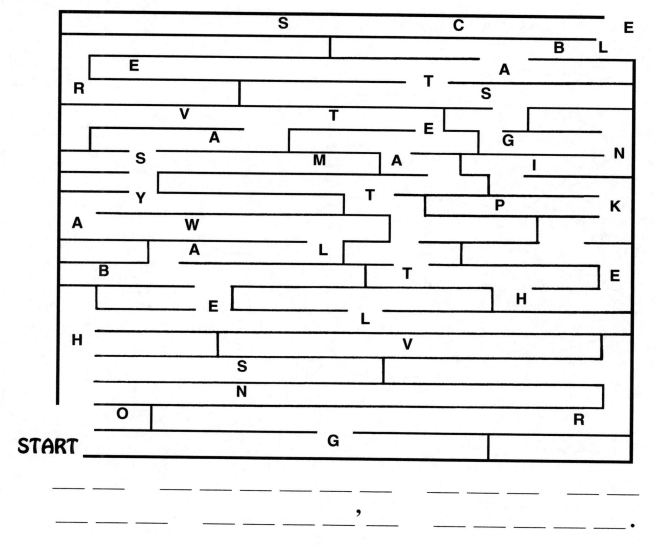

(2 Samuel 9:13)

David and Bathsheba

(2 Samuel 11-12)

Directions: David was a a good king and a godly man, but he was not perfect. To discover his story, follow the path. Begin on the number 1 stone. Flip a coin to see how many steps to move: 2 steps for heads, 1 step for tails. Read the words on the step you land on. *If they are true, move ahead 2 steps. If they are false, move ahead 1 step.* If you do not know, look up the Bible verse in 2 Samuel.

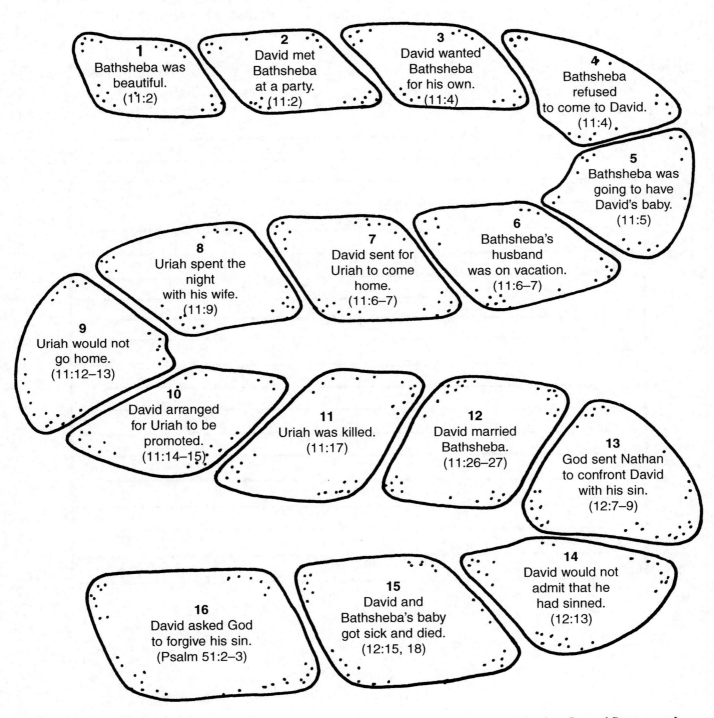

1 Bathsheba was beautiful. (11:2)

2 David met Bathsheba at a party. (11:2)

3 David wanted Bathsheba for his own. (11:4)

4 Bathsheba refused to come to David. (11:4)

5 Bathsheba was going to have David's baby. (11:5)

6 Bathsheba's husband was on vacation. (11:6–7)

7 David sent for Uriah to come home. (11:6–7)

8 Uriah spent the night with his wife. (11:9)

9 Uriah would not go home. (11:12–13)

10 David arranged for Uriah to be promoted. (11:14–15)

11 Uriah was killed. (11:17)

12 David married Bathsheba. (11:26–27)

13 God sent Nathan to confront David with his sin. (12:7–9)

14 David would not admit that he had sinned. (12:13)

15 David and Bathsheba's baby got sick and died. (12:15, 18)

16 David asked God to forgive his sin. (Psalm 51:2–3)

Wicked Absalom

(2 Samuel 14:25–18:18)

David's son Absalom was one of the most handsome men in the whole land, but he had an evil heart. His father loved him, but Absalom loved only himself. He wanted to be king of Israel in place of his father, so he tricked people into thinking he was a great and kind person who would be a good king. Then he took an army of thousands of men to attack David and kill him. David asked his soldiers not to harm his son in the battle. To find out what happened to Absalom, follow the directions.

Directions: In the words below, change every **Z** to **A** and every **Q** to **E**. Then write the hidden message on the lines.

ZS ZBSZLOM'S MULQ WQNT UNDQR THQ

_____

THICK BRZNCHQS OF Z LZRGQ OZK, HIS

_____

HQAD GOT CZUGHT IN THQ TRQQ.   HQ WZS

_____

LQFT HZNGING IN MIDZIR, WHILQ THQ MULQ

_____

KQPT GOING.   WHQN DZVID'S GQNQRZL

_____

SZW ZBSZLOM HZNGING THQRQ, HQ KILLQD HIM.

_____

(2 SAMUEL 18:9, 14)

David Praises God

(2 Samuel 22)

Directions: David knew that he could do nothing without God. He wrote many psalms of praise to God. Read some of David's words of praise below. Then find and circle the underlined words in the word search puzzle.

```
R  A  B  C  Z  L  G  O  D  Q
F  O  R  T  R  E  S  S  E  D
I  P  C  Q  R  E  M  N  L  E
Z  Y  L  K  G  Z  L  E  I  L
L  V  T  U  B  D  I  Z  V  I
C  A  F  D  E  H  G  V  E  G
K  E  M  M  S  G  H  L  R  H
R  J  Z  P  N  R  T  S  E  T
L  R  E  S  C  U  E  D  R  E
S  A  L  V  A  T  I  O  N  D
```

"THE LORD IS MY <u>ROCK</u>, MY <u>FORTRESS</u>, AND MY <u>DELIVERER</u>; MY <u>GOD</u> IS MY ROCK,

IN WHOM I TAKE <u>REFUGE</u>, MY <u>SHIELD</u> AND THE HORN OF MY <u>SALVATION</u>. HE

<u>RESCUED</u> ME BECAUSE HE <u>DELIGHTED</u> IN ME. YOU ARE MY <u>LAMP</u>, O LORD;

THE LORD TURNS MY DARKNESS INTO <u>LIGHT</u>.

(2 Samuel 22:2–3, 20, 29)

King Solomon

(1 Kings 2–3)

When David died after being king of Israel for 40 years, his son Solomon became king. David had given him very good advice about how to be a good king.

Directions: In the word pairs below, one word has a letter that is not in the other word. Write it on the line. Then match the letter to the correct number below to complete what David told Solomon.

1. I'm in GOAT but not in COAT. _____

2. You will find me in SUN but not in FUN. _____

3. You can see me in THAN but not in THEN. _____

4. Here I am in FEED but not in FEEL. _____

5. I am in WALK but not in TALK. _____

6. I appear in SLOW but not in SOW. _____

7. I am twice in NOODLE but not in FEUDAL. _____

8. I can be seen in MEAL but not in SEAL. _____

9. I am in BEAR but not in BAR. _____

10. You can find me in COOK but not in COOL. _____

11. Find me in TRASH but nowhere in CRASH. _____

12. I am in POOL but not in TOOL. _____

13. I am right there in YOUR but not in YOU. _____

14. You can see me in NEEDS but not in SEEDS. _____

David told Solomon, "Be ____ ____ ____ ____ ____ ____, show yourself a
　　　　　　　　　　　2　　11　　13　　7　　14　　1

____ ____ ____, and observe what the ____ ____ ____ ____
8　　3　　14　　　　　　　　　　　　　　6　　7　　13　　4

your God requires: ____ ____ ____ ____ in his ways, and
　　　　　　　　　　　5　　3　　6　　10

____ ____ ____ ____ his decrees and commands." (1 Kings 2:2–3)
10　　9　　9　　12

(1 Kings 5-8)

Directions: King Solomon used the very best materials and thousands of skilled workers to build God's temple. Use the number/letter code to complete some of the temple details.

A	B	C	D	E	F	G	H	I	J	K	L	M
0	1	2	3	4	5	6	7	8	9	10	11	12

N	O	P	Q	R	S	T	U	V	W	X	Y	Z
13	14	15	16	17	18	19	20	21	22	23	24	25

Materials Used

___ ___ ___ ___ ___ and ___ ___ ___ ___ from Lebanon, and ___ ___ ___ ___
2 4 3 0 17   15 8 13 4   6 14 11 3

Workers

___ ___, ___ ___ ___ sent to Lebanon to help cut the wood (1 Kings 5:13)
D A A A A

___ ___, ___ ___ ___ carriers (1 Kings 5:15)
H A A A A

___ ___, ___ ___ ___ stone cutters (1 Kings 5:15)
I A A A A

___, ___ ___ ___ foremen to supervise the work (1 Kings 5:16)
D D A A

Temple Decorations

Solomon had ___ ___ ___ ___ ___ ___, ___ ___ ___ ___ ___ ___ ___, and
0 13 6 4 11 18   5 11 14 22 4 17 18

___ ___ ___ ___ ___ ___ ___ ___ ___ carved on the walls and doors. (1 Kings 6:29)
15 0 11 12 19 17 4 4 18

Time

It took ___ ___ ___ ___ ___ ___ to complete the temple. (1 Kings 6:38))
H 24 4 0 17 18

Great Riches for Solomon

(1 Kings 10)

Directions: God blessed King Solomon with great riches as no one had ever had before. The Queen of Sheba came to visit him and was amazed at what she saw and heard. Read the clues and complete the acrostic with some of Solomon's riches.

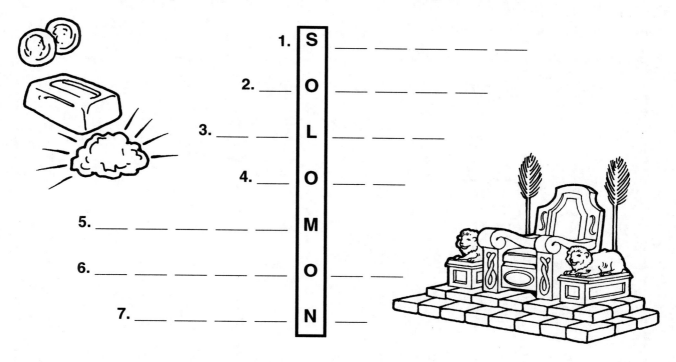

1. **S** __ __ __ __ __

2. __ **O** __ __ __ __

3. __ __ **L** __ __

4. __ **O** __ __

5. __ __ __ __ **M** __ __

6. __ __ __ __ **O** __

7. __ __ __ __ __ **N** __ __

1. Solomon had so much of this, it became as common as stones in Jerusalem. (1 Kings 10:27)

2. The king had 12,000 of these which he kept in Jerusalem and other cities. (1 Kings 10:26

3. Solomon spent 7 years building a beautiful temple for the Lord, but he spent 13 years building this even bigger home for himself. (1 Kings 7:1–2)

4. Every year Solomon received more than 66 talents (25 tons) of this! (1 Kings 10:14)

5. In addition to all his money and possessions, Solomon also had more of this than anyone. (1 Kings 10:23)

6. He owned 1,400 of these. (1 Kings 10:26)

7. Solomon had this king's seat made of ivory and gold. (1 Kings 10:18–19)

A Divided Kingdom

(1 Kings 11–12)

Directions: After all God had done for him, Solomon disobeyed. He married 700 women, many of them from nations that worshiped idols instead of God. He even worshiped the idols with his wives! How did God feel about Solomon's disobedience? To find out what God said, cross out every **C**, **J**, **P**, and **V** in the letter box. Write the remaining letters in order on the lines.

I	J	C	W	I	V	L	P	C	L	T	V	E
J	A	R	T	J	H	P	E	K	I	C	N	G
D	V	O	J	M	P	C	A	W	V	A	J	P
Y	F	J	R	C	O	M	P	Y	V	O	C	V
U	N	V	O	T	C	D	U	J	R	I	P	P
N	G	P	Y	O	C	U	J	R	V	L	I	V
F	J	E	T	C	I	M	V	E	J	B	U	C
T	V	D	U	P	R	V	I	N	C	G	Y	O
V	U	C	R	P	V	S	J	O	V	N	S	V

(1 Kings 11:11–12)

In 930 B.C. after Solomon's death, the kingdom became two kingdoms—Israel in the north and Judah in the south—with two separate kings. This lasted for over 300 years!

Elijah, God's Prophet

(1 Kings 17)

Directions: God had Elijah warn King Ahab that there was going to be a drought throughout Israel. Then God sent Elijah to stay near a brook where ravens fed him. When the brook dried up, God sent Elijah to a poor woman with one son. To discover the miracle Elijah did for her, connect the letters that spell ELIJAH GODS PROPHET. Then write the remaining letters in order on the lines.

E	H	I	E	R	J	A
R	L	O	J	F	F	L
O	U	R	A	H	W	A
S	N	O	O	G	T	U
S	E	S	D	☆	D	U
P	A	☆	P	R	N	D
H	E	R	J	O	U	G
O	F	O	P	I	L	D
I	D	H	E	N	O	T
D	R	T	Y	U	P	☆

___ ___ ___ ___ ___ ___ ___ ___ ___ ___ ___ ___ ___

___ ___ ___ ___ ___ ___ ___ ___ ___

___ ___ ___ ___ ___ ___ ___ ___ ___ ___

___ ___ ___ ___ ___ ___ ___ ___

___ ___ ___ ___ ___ ___ ___ ___ ___. (1 Kings 17:16)

A Contest on Mount Carmel

(1 Kings 18)

Directions: Elijah challenged King Ahab to a contest on Mount Carmel. Ahab's idol-worshiping prophets would compete with Elijah's God. Ahab's prophets put a bull on their altar and shouted to their god all morning to burn up their offering, but nothing happened. Then it was Elijah's turn. Look at the pictures for the rest of the story. Number them from 1 to 6 to show in what order they happened.

_____ Elijah asked God to show His power to all the people.

_____ The people cried out, "The Lord—he is God!"

_____ Elijah built an altar and put a bull on it.

_____ Fire came down and burned up the offering and licked up the water in the trench.

_____ Elijah poured 12 jars of water on the offering until it spilled over and filled the trench.

_____ Elijah dug a deep trench around the altar.

Directions: Decode the words below; then use them to complete the story.

Main Characters:

☆ ✳ ☆ ✻ ____

♠ ☆ ✻ ♣ ◆ ✳ ____

◆ ✳ ♣ ✳ ✻ ✳ ◇ ____

✳ ◇ ✢ ◆ ☆ ✳ ____

Places:

✳ ☆ ◇ ☆ ☆ ✳ ____

✳ ✢ ♠ ✳ ✚ ☆ ✛ ✳ ____

Actions:

☆ ★ ✛ ✡ ✳ ✳ ____

✡ ◆ ✿ ♠ ✳ ✳ ____

```
CODE
A       B       C       D       E
☆       ✻       ☆       ✳       ✳

F       H       I       J       L
✶       ✳       ✢       ◆       ◇

N       O       P       R       S
♠       ♣       ✳       ✛       ✡

T       U       V       W       Y       Z
◆       ★       ✳       ✢       ✚       ♣
```

____ ____ ____ ____ saw a ____ ____ ____ ____ ____ ____ ____ ____ he wanted for his own,

but ____ ____ ____ ____ ____ ____, the owner, would not sell it. ____ ____ ____ ____ went

home to his ____ ____ ____ ____ ____ ____ and pouted. When his wicked wife,

____ ____ ____ ____ ____ ____ ____ , found out what was wrong, she promised to take care of

it for him. She arranged for the leaders of the town where ____ ____ ____ ____ ____ ____ lived

to accuse him of blasphemey in front of the people. Two evil men falsely testified that

____ ____ ____ ____ ____ ____ had ____ ____ ____ ____ ____ ____ God. Then he was

____ ____ ____ ____ ____ ____ ____. ____ ____ ____ ____ happily went to take possession

of his new property. But ____ ____ ____ ____ ____ ____ was there to meet him. He told

the king that God was going to bring disaster on him and his family because of what he had done.

Elijah Goes to Heaven

(2 Kings 2)

Directions: Elijah, God's prophet, did not die and go to heaven in the usual way. To discover the fantastic way he left this earth, cross out the letters that spell HEAVEN in each group of letters. Write the remaining letters on the lines, working left to right, to complete each sentence. Then draw a picture to show how you think this unusual event looked.

H C E H A A R V I E O N T   **H E F A I V R E E N**

H H O E R A S V E E N S   **H F E A I R V E N E**

H W H E I R A L W V I E N N D

Elijah went to heaven in a ___ ___ ___ ___ ___ ___ ___ of

___ ___ ___ ___ pulled by ___ ___ ___ ___ ___ ___ ___ of ___ ___ ___ ___

in a ___ ___ ___ ___ ___ ___ ___ ___! (2 Kings 2:11)

Elisha's Miracles

(2 Kings 2:19–22; 4:1–44)

Directions: God gave Elisha power to perform many miracles. Solve each riddle. Then match each answer to the correct miracle.

RIDDLES

A. Shake a little on your meal

to give it flavor with real appeal.

_____

B. A pole made of wood

it did what it should.

_____

C. Made from olives and used for everything

from cooking to rubbing on hurts that sting.

_____

D. A substance for making

foods needing baking.

_____

E. Food for everyone

in a loaf or a bun.

_____

MIRACLES

_____ **1.** Elisha brought a woman's son back to life.
(2 Kings 4:29–31, 35)

_____ **2.** Elisha made bad water drinkable. (2 Kings 2:21–22)

_____ **3.** Elisha fed 100 men with just a little of this.
(2 Kings 4:42–44)

_____ **4.** A poor woman borrowed many jars from her neighbors and they were all filled with this. She sold the filled jars to pay her debts.
(2 Kings 4:3–4)

_____ **5.** Elisha made a poisonous pot of stew safe to eat.
(2 Kings 4:41)

Naaman's Leprosy Is Healed

(2 Kings 5:1-16)

Directions: Naaman was an army commander, a proud and brave soldier who had a big problem! He had leprosy, a terrible disease for which there was no cure. Elisha told him an unusual way to be cured. To discover the cure, cross out all the double letters in the words in the box. Then use the words to complete what Elisha told Naaman.

```
W E E A S H P P          K K J O L L R D I I A N

F L O O E S B B H        R E C C S T E E O R E D

R R S E V Z Z E N        R S S I J J V E R

          Z Z C L A A E A N M M S E D
```

Elisha told Naaman,

"Go, _____ yourself

_____ times

in the _____ _____

and your _____

will be _____ and you

will be _____." (2 Kings 5:10)

It sounded so crazy, Naaman was almost too proud to do it, but his servants convinced him to try. And he was glad he did because he was cured completely!

Elisha and the Arameans

(2 Kings 6:8–23)

The king of Aram sent a big part of his army to capture Elisha. The soldiers with horses and chariots completely surrounded the city where Elisha was staying. "What shall we do?" his frightened servant asked. To find out what happened, follow the directions.

Directions: In the words below, change every **Z** to **E**, every **J** to **O**, and every **X** to **R**. Then illustrate it below. Read the rest of this exciting story in 2 Kings 6.

ELISHA SAID, "D J N'T BZ AFXAID. THJSZ WHJ AXZ WITH US

_____

AXZ MJXZ THAN THJSZ WHJ AXZ WITH THZM."

_____

THZN GJD JPZNZD THZ SZXVANT'S ZYZS AND

_____

HZ SAW THZ HILLS FULL JF HJRSZS AND

_____

CHARIJTS JF FIXZ AXJUND ZLISHA.

_____

(2 Kings 6:16–17)

King Joash

(2 Kings 11)

Ahaziah was an evil king of Judah. When he died, the next king should have been his son Joash. But Joash's grandmother planned to kill him so she could make herself queen. His aunt hid him in the temple for six years while his wicked grandmother ruled the land. When Joash was seven years old, the temple priest and other supporters took him from the temple and crowned him king of Judah. (His grandmother was killed.)

Directions: Help Joash find his way through the maze from the temple to the king's palace.

King's Palace

Joash

King Hezekiah's Prayer

(2 Kings 20)

Hezekiah, a godly king of Judah, was very sick, about to die. He prayed to the Lord, and the Lord sent His prophet Isaiah to tell him he would recover. Hezekiah wanted a sign to prove that God was going to heal him. To discover a description of Hezekiah's faith and the sign God gave him, follow the directions.

Directions: Write all the words in the number 1 boxes in order on the number 1 line, all the words in the number 2 boxes on the number 2 line, and so on until you have used all the words.

GO 4	DID 2	HE 1	HAD 5	THE 3
LORD 3	GONE 5	BACK 4	NOT 2	MADE 3
HELD 1	DOWN 5	THE 3	FAST 1	THE 4
ON 5	CEASE 2	TO 1	TEN 4	TO 2
FOLLOW 2	STEPS 4	THE 5	HIM 2	THE 1
STAIRWAY 5	LORD 1	IT 4	SHADOW 3	AND 1

Hezekiah's Faith

1. _____

2. _____

God's Sign

3. _____

4. _____

5. _____

Josiah, the Boy King

(2 Kings 22–23)

Directions: Josiah was only eight years old when he became king of Judah, but he did what was right and followed God. He did three very important things while he was king. To find out what they were, choose a word from the box below to solve the clues. Then write the answers in the box at the bottom of the page.

ordered	people	celebrate	book	people
Passover	repaired	temple	covenant	read

CLUES

1. This is another word for "fixed"—when something breaks, it needs to be _____.

2. This was the building where Jews worshiped God. _____

3. This is what you do to your favorite book. (You use your eyes to do this.) _____

4. This is a story of many pages between covers. _____

5. This is a Bible word for an agreement between God and people. It starts with the letter C.
   _____

6. This is a word for men and women and boys and girls of all ages. _____

7. This is another word for "told" or "commanded." _____

8. This is a word for men and women and boys and girls of all ages. _____

9. The reason we have birthday parties is to _____.

10. This is a Bible holiday for Jews to help them remember how God brought them out of Egypt.
    _____

WHAT JOSIAH DID

He _____ the _____.
      1   2

He _____ the _____
      3   4

of the _____ to the _____.
      5   6

He _____ the _____ to
      7   8

_____
      9

the _____.
      10

Going Home

(Ezra 1-10)

For 70 years most of the Jewish people had been living as captives in the lands of those who conquered them. But God had not forgotten them. He moved the heart of the King of Persia to free any Jews who wanted to go home and rebuild their temple. Almost 30,000 people returned to the homeland and began working on the temple in Jerusalem. Later, another king sent more Jews home, including Ezra, a Bible teacher. Ezra helped the Jews see that they had been disobeying God by marrying ungoldy, idol-worshiping people of other lands. Follow the directions to discover what Ezra prayed for the people.

Directions: In the word box below, cross out all of the following: even numbers, colors, words that begin with **L**, and words that end in **W**. Then write the remaining words in order on the lines.

WHAT	WHITE	HAS	TWO	HAPPENED	TWENTY
TO	SIX	US	LET	IS	A
RESULT	SAW	OF	OUR	FLOW	EVIL
HOW	DEEDS	LONG	NOW	AND	LOW
OUR	LAST	GREAT	GUILT	GREEN	HERE
WE	FOUR	ARE	BEFORE	LORD	FEW
YOU	IN	LISTEN	OUR	KNOW	GUILT
THOUGH	BECAUSE	BLUE	OF	TEN	IT
NOT	ONE	LESS	OF	RENEW	US
CAN	BOW	STAND	BROWN	LEFT	IN
RED	FORTY	YOUR	GROW	EIGHT	PRESENCE

_____ _____ _____ _____ _____ _____ _____

_____ _____ _____ _____ _____ _____

_____ _____ _____ _____ _____ _____ .

_____ _____ _____ _____ _____ _____

_____ _____ , _____ _____ _____

_____ _____ _____ _____ _____ .

_____ _____ _____ _____ .

(Ezra 9:13a, 15b)

Nehemiah Rebuilds the Wall

(Nehemiah 1-6)

When other nations conquered the Jews, they broke down the wall around Jerusalem. More than 70 years later Jews were being allowed to go back to their homeland. Nehemiah got permission from the king he worked for to go to Jerusalem to get the city wall rebuilt. It was not easy. First, Nehemiah had to convince the people to do the work. Then he had to encourage the workers and help them ignore the insults of enemies. They had to work with a weapon in one hand to guard against enemy attack.

Directions: To find out how long it took to rebuild the wall, connect the odd numbers from the smallest to the largest in the number maze. Then add up the remaining numbers.

1	2	5	6	2
4	3	9	11	2
2	27	19	4	13
39	35	2	15	4
2	47	4	65	6
2	4	51	4	71
131	123	99	91	2

It took _____ days to rebuild the wall around Jerusalem.

(Nehemiah 6:15)

Brave Queen Esther

(Esther 1-10)

Directions: Esther was a young Jewish girl, a captive in a foreign land. But because of her beauty she was chosen to be queen. God used her to protect her people from Haman, a wicked man who hated all Jews because of one Jew named Mordecai who would not bow down to him. Find and circle the words from the story in the word search puzzle.

ESTHER
MORDECAI
XERXES
HAMAN
PALACE
CROWN
QUEEN
BANQUET
JEWS
DESTROY
SCEPTER

E	X	E	R	X	E	S	D	F	M
O	S	P	A	L	A	C	E	R	O
S	U	T	S	Q	C	E	S	C	R
H	A	W	H	U	T	P	T	R	D
I	E	M	E	E	A	T	R	O	E
J	S	T	H	E	R	E	O	W	C
H	A	M	A	N	I	R	Y	N	A
S	?	B	A	N	Q	U	E	T	I

Directions: Write the remaining letters on the lines below to complete what Mordecai told Esther about God's plan for her life.

Who knows but that you have come to royal position

___ ___ ___   ___ ___ ___ ___ ___ ___   ___   ___ ___ ___ ___

___ ___   ___ ___ ___ ___   ___   (Esther 4:14b)

Job's Troubles

(Job 1-2)

Directions: Job had many troubles in his life, but he remained true to the Lord. Unscramble the sentences to find out what Job said when he was suffering. (*Hint:* To help you, the letter and number under each line tell the first letter of the word and the number of letters it has.)

THAT   LIVES   AND   I   END   MY   WILL   GOD   I   SKIN   STAND

REDEEMER   IN   WILL   HE   KNOW   THAT   SEE   MY   THE   UPON   THE

AND   YET   HAS   BEEN   MY   IN   FLESH   AFTER   EARTH   DESTROYED

____ I-1   _____ K-4   _____ T-4   _____ M-2

_____ R-8   _____ L-5 ,   _____ A-3

_____ T-4   _____ I-2   _____ T-3   _____ E-3   _____ H-2

_____ W-4   _____ S-5   _____ U-4   _____ T-3

_____ E-5 .   _____ A-3   _____ A-5   _____ M-2

_____ S-4   _____ H-3   _____ B-4   _____ D-9 ,

_____ Y-3   _____ I-2   _____ M-2   _____ F-5   ____ I-1

_____ W-4   _____ S-3   _____ G-3 . (Job 19:25–26)

Isaiah, Prophet of Judgment

(Isaiah 1–3)

Directions: God's people had been ignoring Him and were worshiping idols. God sent His prophet Isaiah to tell them that He was going to punish them if they did not leave their idols and return to the Lord. Solve the math problems. Then choose the numbered words to discover what Isaiah said.

RIGHTEOUS 24	WELL 10	DEEDS 7	WOE 5	UPON 9	FOR 2
TELL 4	WICKED 12	DISASTER 19	THE 8	FRUIT 16	BE 21
TO 3	WILL 11	THEM 20	THEIR 14	IT 6	THEY 17
WITH 15	OF 13	IS 18	ENJOY 22		

_____ $2 \times 2 =$ _____ $4 + 4 =$ _____ $6 \times 4 =$ _____ $18 - 12 =$

_____ $13 - 2 =$ _____ $7 \times 3 =$ _____ $5 \times 2 =$ _____ $10 + 5 =$ _____ $25 - 5 =$,

_____ $8 - 6 =$ _____ $10 + 7 =$ _____ $22 - 11 =$ _____ $10 + 12 =$

_____ $17 - 9 =$ _____ $8 \times 2 =$ _____ $6 + 7 =$ _____ $2 \times 7 =$

_____ $19 - 12 =$. _____ $4 + 1 =$ _____ $9 - 6 =$ _____ $15 - 7 =$

_____ $4 \times 3 =$! _____ $21 - 2 =$ _____ $9 \times 2 =$

_____ $5 + 4 =$ _____ $40 - 20 =$! (Isaiah 3:10–11)

Jeremiah in Danger

(Jeremiah 26)

God told His prophet Jeremiah to warn the people of Judah that He was going to punish them if they did not stop sinning and turn back to Him. Some people got so angry at his message, they grabbed Jeremiah and said he should be put to death! Did Jeremiah back down? Did they scare him into changing his message? To find out, follow the directions.

Directions: To decode what Jeremiah said, change every **J** to **E**, every **Q** to **A**, and every **Z** to **N**.

RJFORM YOUR WQYS QZD YOUR QCTIOZS QZD OBJY

_____

THJ LORD YOUR GOD. THJZ THJ LORD WILL RJLJZT

_____

QZD ZOT BRIZG THJ DISQSTJR HJ HQS PROZOUZCJD

_____

QGQIZST YOU. QS FOR MJ, I QM IZ YOUR HQZDS; DO

_____

WITH MJ WHQTJVJR YOU THIZK IS GOOD QZD RIGHT.

_____

(Jeremiah 26:13–14)

To find out what happened to Jeremiah, read Jeremiah 26:16, 24.

Ezekiel's Vision of Dry Bones

(Ezekiel 37)

Directions: Sometimes God spoke to His prophets through visions. Ezekiel had a strange one. Complete the clues; then write the correct clue word on each numbered line.

CLUES

1. Opposite of "wet" ____ ____ ____

2. The covering on our bodies ____ ____ ____ ____

3. Opposite of "women" ____ ____ ____

4. Where we plant plants ____ ____ ____ ____ ____ ____

5. What our skeleton is made of ____ ____ ____ ____ ____

6. Opposite of dead ____ ____ ____ ____ ____ ____

7. A large group of soliders ____ ____ ____ ____

8. Listened ____ ____ ____ ____ ____

9. Noise ____ ____ ____ ____ ____

10. Opposite of "separate" ____ ____ ____ ____ ____ ____ ____ ____

Ezekiel saw ____ ____ ____   ____ ____ ____ ____ ____ on the
                1   5

____ ____ ____ ____ ____ ____. Then he ____ ____ ____ ____ ____ a rattling
         4   8

____ ____ ____ ____ ____, and the ____ ____ ____ ____ ____ came
        9   5

____ ____ ____ ____ ____ ____ ____. Then ____ ____ ____ ____ covered
        10   2

them and they became a ____ ____ ____ ____ ____   ____ ____ ____ ____
                          6   7

of ____ ____ ____.
      3

God used this vision to explain that He would give life back to

His people by bringing them back to Israel.

Daniel and His Three Friends

(Daniel 1)

Directions: When King Nebuchadnezzar conquered Jerusalem, he took many of the people as captives back to his own land. Daniel and three of his friends were among those captives taken from their homeland. Complete their story, using words from the number/letter box.

1	C	G	M	R
2	A	T	K	V
3	N	D	B	H
4	E	O	Y	L
5	S	W	Z	I
	6	7	8	9

Daniel and his friends were to be trained with others to serve in the king's palace. First, Daniel's

name was changed to ___ ___ ___ ___ ___ ___ ___ ___ ___ ___ ___,
　　　　　　　　　　　　 3-8 4-6 4-9 2-7 4-6 5-6 3-9 2-6 5-8 5-8 2-6 1-9

Hananiah became ___ ___ ___ ___ ___ ___ ___ ___, Mishael became
　　　　　　　　　　 5-6 3-9 2-6 3-7 1-9 2-6 1-6 3-9

___ ___ ___ ___ ___ ___ ___, and Azariah became
1-8 4-6 5-6 3-9 2-6 1-6 3-9

___ ___ ___ ___ ___ ___ ___ ___. When the boys being trained were given
2-6 3-8 4-6 3-7 3-6 4-6 1-7 4-7

royal food and wine, Daniel and his friends chose instead to drink ___ ___ ___ ___ ___ and
　　　　　　　　　　　　　　　　　　　　　　　　　　　　　　　　 5-7 2-6 2-7 4-6 1-9

eat ___ ___ ___ ___ ___ ___ ___ ___ ___ ___. They became healthier than the
　　 2-9 4-6 1-7 4-6 2-7 2-6 3-8 4-9 4-6 5-6

others. God also blessed them and gave them ___ ___ ___ ___ ___ ___ ___ ___ ___
　　　　　　　　　　　　　　　　　　　　　　　　　 2-8 3-6 4-7 5-7 4-9 4-6 3-7 1-7 4-6

and understanding. At the end of the training period, the king questioned all the boys and found Daniel

and his friends not only healthier, but ___ ___ ___ times smarter than even his own magicians!
　　　　　　　　　　　　　　　　　　　　 2-7 4-6 3-6

The Fiery Furnace

(Daniel 3)

King Nebuchadnezzar made a huge image of gold, then commanded that everyone must bow down and worship it. Anyone who did not would be thrown into a blazing furnace. Shadrach, Meshach, and Abednego refused to do it. The king was furious and had the furnace made seven times hotter! Then the three men were thrown into the fiery furnace. He was amazed to see that the flames did not harm them and that there were four men in the furnace! When the three friends were brought out of the furnace, they were not burnt at all; their clothes did not even smell like smoke. What they had told the king was proved true.

Directions: To find out what they told him, circle the words from the story in the word search puzzle. Then write the leftover letters on the lines below the puzzle.

SHADRACH

MESHACH

ABEDNEGO

FURNACE

KING

IMAGE

GOLD

FURIOUS

SEVEN

FOUR

A	B	E	D	N	E	G	O	S
T	F	U	R	I	O	U	S	H
H	E	U	G	O	D	K	W	A
F	O	U	R	E	S	I	E	D
R	V	E	D	N	I	N	S	R
S	A	L	I	M	A	G	E	A
B	O	L	E	T	O	C	V	C
G	S	A	V	E	U	S	E	H
M	E	S	H	A	C	H	N	H

__ __ __ __   __ __ __ __ __ __   __ __ __ __   __ __ __ __

__ __ __   __ __ __ __ __   __ __ __   __ __ __ __ __ __   __ __ __!

(Daniel 3:17)

A Message on a Wall

(Daniel 5)

King Belshazzar was a wicked king. During a big party, he decided to show off by drinking wine from gold cups from God's temple. He did not believe in God, but what happened next made him change his mind. To find out what happened, follow the directions.

Directions: Cross out all words in the box that begin with **B**, **C**, **N**, and **S**. Write the remaining words on the lines.

THE	BIBLE	FINGERS	NOT	OF	A	STAND	HUMAN
HAND	BODY	APPEARED	AND	CHANGED	WROTE	ON	NICE
THE	PLASTER	START	BOX	OF	CALL	SHE	THE
WALL	SURE	IT	WAS	BREAK	A	NEVER	MESSAGE
BEGIN	FROM	GOD	CASE	THAT	THE	STILL	KING
WAS	CAN	GOING	BE	TO	BEAT	DIE	NO

_____   _____   _____

_____   _____   _____

_____   _____   _____   ____

_____   _____.   _____   _____

_____   _____   _____   _____

_____   _____   _____.

Daniel and the Den of Lions

(Daniel 6)

Directions: Read the story of Daniel and the lions. Then fit the underlined words from the story into the crossword puzzle.

> Daniel worked for the king, but his co-workers were jealous of him. They tricked the king and got Daniel arrested because he prayed to God three times every day. Daniel spent the night with a den of lions. He was not hurt because God sent an angel to shut the lions' mouths.

Jonah and the Big Fish

(Jonah 1–4)

Directions: Jonah tried to run from God when he did not want to do what he was told. But he could not hide from God. Use words from the circle to complete the story.

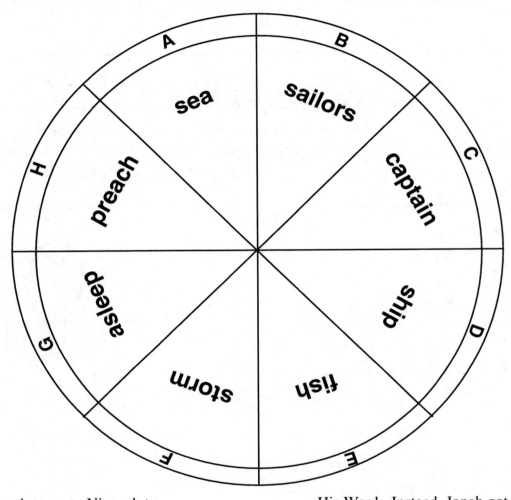

God told Jonah to go to Nineveh to _____ His Word. Instead, Jonah got on a
                                        H

_____ and went in the opposite direction. Suddenly, a terrible _____ began
      D   F

battering the _____. The _____ thought they were going to drown. The
                    D   B

_____ found Jonah _____. "Get up and call on your god to save us!"
          C   G

he said. Jonah knew the _____ was from God, so he told them to throw him overboard
                                F

and it would stop. They did not want to, but they tossed Jonah into the _____ where a big
                                                                              A

_____ swallowed him whole. For three days and nights inside that _____
      E   E

Jonah prayed until God had the fish spit him out on dry ground. Then Jonah hurried toward Nineveh.

An Angel Visits Mary and Joseph

(Matthew 1:18–25; Luke 1:26–38)

It was amazing! Mary and Joseph, her future husband, both had visits from an angel. And the angel had the same important message from God for each of them. To find the message, follow the directions.

Directions: Cross out all the following letters in the boxes: **C, F, K, P, Q,** and **Z.** Write the remaining letters in order on the lines below.

M	A	C	R	Z	Y	W	P	Q
I	L	F	L	G	F	I	C	V
Z	E	B	Q	I	Z	R	T	F
H	K	T	P	O	A	S	Z	O
F	F	N	A	Q	N	D	Y	C
Z	O	U	A	C	R	E	T	P
O	K	N	A	M	Q	E	H	I
Z	M	J	E	K	S	U	F	S

___ ___ ___   ___ ___ ___   ___ ___ ___   ___ ___ ___

___ ___ ___ ___   ___ ___ ___   ___   ___ ___ ___,

___ ___ ___   ___ ___ ___   ___ ___ ___ ___ ___

___ ___ ___   ___ ___ ___   ___ ___ ___ ___ ___ .

Jesus' Birth

(Luke 2:1-20)

Directions: Solve the riddles. Then use your answers to complete the story of the birth of Jesus.

RIDDLES

1. People traveling stopped to stay
in this motel of an earlier day.

_____

2. They were messengers from God to man,
praising Him for His perfect plan.

_____

3. Animals had eaten food from this bin
that became a bed for a child to lie in.

_____

4. Chosen by God, this girl was the one
who became the mother of His only Son.

_____

5. Suddenly wakened from their sleep,
they heard good news and left their sheep.

_____

6. This shed where dirty animals stayed
became the place where God's Son lay.

_____

7. Their keepers suddenly left them and ran,
but why they could not understand.

_____

8. He was the one who sent His Son
to be born and die for everyone.

_____

STORY

Joseph and _____ traveled to Bethlehem to register for the census.

The _____ was full, so they spent the night in a _____

where animals were kept. Jesus was born there and his mother laid him in a

_____ to sleep. _____ announced His birth first to

_____ caring for their _____ in nearby fields. They

found the baby, then praised _____ and told everyone about Jesus.

Important Visitors to Bethlehem

(Matthew 2:1-12)

Wise men, also called *magi*, came to find Jesus. They stopped in Jerusalem and asked, "Where is the one who has been born king of the Jews?" King Herod called on the chief priests and teachers of the Law to find the answer. They found it in the Old Testament.

Directions: Choose words from the box to complete the verse they read and to answer the question below. One word will be used twice.

Jerusalem	Israel	Judah	sheep
forever	ruler	shepherd	servant
people	Bethlehem	land	Micah
John	king	Nazareth	city

"But you, _____, in the _____ of

_____, are by no means least among the rulers of

_____; for out of you will come a _____

who will be the _____ of my _____

_____." (Matthew 2:6)

What old Testament Minor Prophet said this? _____

John the Baptist

(Matthew 3:1–17)

Directions: John the Baptist spent his time preaching and telling people, "Repent, for the kingdom of heaven is near." Solve the math problems to complete the code. Then decode the words to find out how people responded to John's preaching.

CODE

A: $7 + 2 =$ _____   G: $17 + 2 =$ _____   N: $4 + 8 =$ _____   T: $9 + 7 =$ _____

B: $5 + 2 =$ _____   H: $14 - 13 =$ _____   O: $28 - 14 =$ _____   V: $25 - 4 =$ _____

C: $11 - 7 =$ _____   I: $24 - 19 =$ _____   P: $7 + 13 =$ _____   W: $13 - 7 =$ _____

D: $3 + 5 =$ _____   J: $7 + 3 =$ _____   R: $6 + 5 =$ _____   Y: $4 + 9 =$ _____

E: $12 - 9 =$ _____   M: $9 + 9 =$ _____   S: $13 - 11 =$ _____   Z: $21 - 4 =$ _____

F: $21 - 6 =$ _____

$\overline{}_{4}\ \overline{}_{14}\ \overline{}_{12}\ \overline{}_{15}\ \overline{}_{3}\ \overline{}_{2}\ \overline{}_{2}\ \overline{}_{5}\ \overline{}_{12}\ \overline{}_{19}\qquad \overline{}_{16}\ \overline{}_{1}\ \overline{}_{3}\ \overline{}_{5}\ \overline{}_{11}$

$\overline{}_{2}\ \overline{}_{5}\ \overline{}_{12}\ \overline{}_{2},\quad \overline{}_{16}\ \overline{}_{1}\ \overline{}_{3}\ \overline{}_{13}\qquad \overline{}_{6}\ \overline{}_{3}\ \overline{}_{11}\ \overline{}_{3}$

$\overline{}_{7}\ \overline{}_{9}\ \overline{}_{20}\ \overline{}_{16}\ \overline{}_{5}\ \overline{}_{17}\ \overline{}_{3}\ \overline{}_{8}\qquad \overline{}_{7}\ \overline{}_{13}\qquad \overline{}_{1}\ \overline{}_{5}\ \overline{}_{18}\qquad \overline{}_{5}\ \overline{}_{12}$

$\overline{}_{16}\ \overline{}_{1}\ \overline{}_{3}\qquad \overline{}_{10}\ \overline{}_{14}\ \overline{}_{11}\ \overline{}_{8}\ \overline{}_{9}\ \overline{}_{12}\qquad \overline{}_{11}\ \overline{}_{5}\ \overline{}_{21}\ \overline{}_{3}\ \overline{}_{11}.$

(Matthew 3:6)

Jesus' First Miracle

(John 2:1-11)

Directions: Complete the story of Jesus' miracle at Cana by writing the missing words in the acrostic.

1. **W** ___ ___ ___
2. ___ **E** ___ ___ ___ ___ ___ ___
3. **D** ___ ___ ___ ___ ___ ___ ___ ___
4. **D** ___
5. ___ **I** ___ ___ ___
6. ___ ___ ___ **N** ___
7. **G** ___ ___ ___ ___
8. ___ **A** ___ ___
9. ___ ___ **T** ___ ___ ___
10. **C** ___ ___ ___ ___ ___ ___
11. ___ **A** ___ ___ ___ ___
12. ___ ___ **N** ___ ___ ___ ___
13. ___ **A** ___ ___ ___

Jesus, His __3__ , and His __9__ went to a wedding in the town of Cana. Before the __12__ was over, they ran out of __1__ . Jesus' mother wanted Him to do something about it. She told the __2__ , " __4__ whatever he tells you." Jesus pointed to six __6__ __8__ . He told them to fill them with __13__ . They did what He said, and when they began serving it, it had become good __1__ . The __11__ of the banquet was amazed that the bridegroom had saved his __10__ __1__ for later in the meal. He did not know that it was miracle __1__ ! This was Jesus' __5__ miracle, revealing His __7__ and making His __3__ put their faith in Him.

Jesus' Sermon on the Mount

(Matthew 5)

Directions: Jesus sat down on a mountainside with His disciples gathered around Him. Crowds of people stood as close as possible to hear what He would say. Most were hoping to see Him perform a miracle. Unscramble the Beatitude words below (the numbers will help you) and write the words on the line. Then match them with the correct endings at the bottom of the page. One ending will be used twice.

Blessed are:

___ **1.** the R O O P   N I   S T R I P I _____
  4 3 2 1   2 1   1 6 4 3 2 5

___ **2.** those who O R M N U _____
  2 4 1 5 3

___ **3.** the K E M E _____
  4 2 1 3

___ **4.** those who G E R N U H and H T I R T S for O G E U S H R I T S N E S
  4 5 6 3 2 1   2 1 3 4 6 5   7 3 6 8 9 4 1 2 5 13 10 11 12

_____

___ **5.** the I R U L F M E C _____
  5 3 7 8 6 1 2 4

___ **6.** the P R E U   N I   T H E R A _____
  1 3 4 2   2 1   5 1 2 4 3

___ **7.** the S E R A K M E C A E P _____
  11 9 10 7 8 6 5 4 3 2 1

___ **8.** those who are S E R T E P E C U D   E B C U A E S   F O
  4 5 3 8 9 1 2 6 7 10   2 1 3 5 4 7 6   2 1

  G H T R I O U E S S N E S _____
  3 4 5 1 2 7 8 6 9 13 10 11 12

_____

A. for they will be called sons of God

B. for they will be filled

C. for theirs is the kingdom of heaven

D. for they will be comforted

E. for they will see God

F. for they will inherit the earth

G. for they will be shown mercy

Jesus' Teaching on Prayer

(Matthew 6)

Directions: Jesus gave His followers a pattern for prayer. He did not say we should pray just that exact prayer all the time. Sometimes he wants us to use our own words but have the same ideas in our prayers. Read the Lord's Prayer in the box below the way we usually say it. Then decode the words to rewrite His prayer in our everyday language.

CODE

A = B	D = C	E = F	H = G	I = J	N = M
O = L	P = Q	R = U	S = V	T = W	

> Our Father which art in heaven, Hallowed be thy name. Thy kingdom come. Thy will be done in earth, as it is in heaven. Give us this day our daily bread. And forgive us our debts, as we forgive our debtors. And lead us not into temptation, but deliver us from evil: For thine is the kingdom, and the power, and the glory, forever.
>
> (Matthew 6:9–13, KJV)

Father, we ___ ___ ___ ___ ___ and ___ ___ ___ ___ ___ ___
           G   L   M   L   U   Q   U   B   J   V   F

your name. Let your will be done here on earth as it is done in heaven.

Provide our ___ ___ ___ ___ ___ today. Forgive our
             M   F   F   C   V

___ ___ ___ ___ and help us to forgive people who ___ ___ ___
 V   J   M   V   V   J   M

against us. Help us to ___ ___ ___ ___ ___ ___ temptation, and
                         U   F   V   J   V   W

not give in to ___ ___ ___ ___ ___. You are our great God,
                 V   B   W   B   M

all powerful, and in control of everything forever.

The Woman at the Well

(John 4:1-42)

Directions: One day Jesus talked to a Samaritan woman at a well. Meeting Him changed her life forever. Cross out all the **Xs** in the puzzle; then write the remaining letters in order on the lines to discover what Jesus told the woman.

W	X	X	H	O	X	X
X	E	V	E	X	R	D
X	R	X	I	X	N	X
K	S	T	X	H	X	E
W	X	A	T	X	E	R
I	X	G	I	X	V	X
E	H	I	X	M	W	I
X	L	L	N	X	E	V
E	X	R	T	X	H	X
X	I	X	R	X	S	T

_____ _____ _____ _____   _____ _____ _____ _____ _____ _____

_____ _____ _____ _____ _____ _____ _____ _____ _____

_____ _____ _____ _____ _____ _____. (John 4: 14)

The Centurion's Servant

(Luke 7:1-10)

Directions: A centurion, a Roman soldier, asked Jesus to heal his servant. When Jesus met the soldier, He was amazed. To find out what amazed Jesus about the man, color all the boxes below that have even numbers in them.

3	7	19	5	12	9	16	23	2	11	8	4	20	21	7	3	5
17	13	99	41	6	13	24	33	22	9	44	21	109	77	99	1	9
15	11	7	43	2	32	16	9	48	7	60	88	46	9	5	43	11
19	3	11	1	8	13	4	5	14	21	23	75	18	33	19	7	9
5	103	15	9	10	7	88	93	28	5	2	12	42	73	9	3	1
53	39	77	49	97	5	17	3	91	87	51	35	5	21	1	5	5
10	2	14	33	42	4	12	19	20	67	64	20	8	15	88	75	4
12	7	1	99	26	5	18	15	76	103	25	6	59	31	36	7	8
22	44	66	47	40	6	14	1	10	79	53	80	49	3	24	12	6
80	77	3	15	6	87	82	29	4	37	91	62	55	5	36	41	10
100	53	71	9	2	73	30	39	18	29	67	12	37	29	14	15	64

Jesus at Peter's House

(Matthew 8:14–17)

Directions: Jesus went to Peter's house and did a miracle there. To find out who he helped and what happened, starting at the arrow, write every other word from the box on the lines below. Then answer the question in the middle of the box.

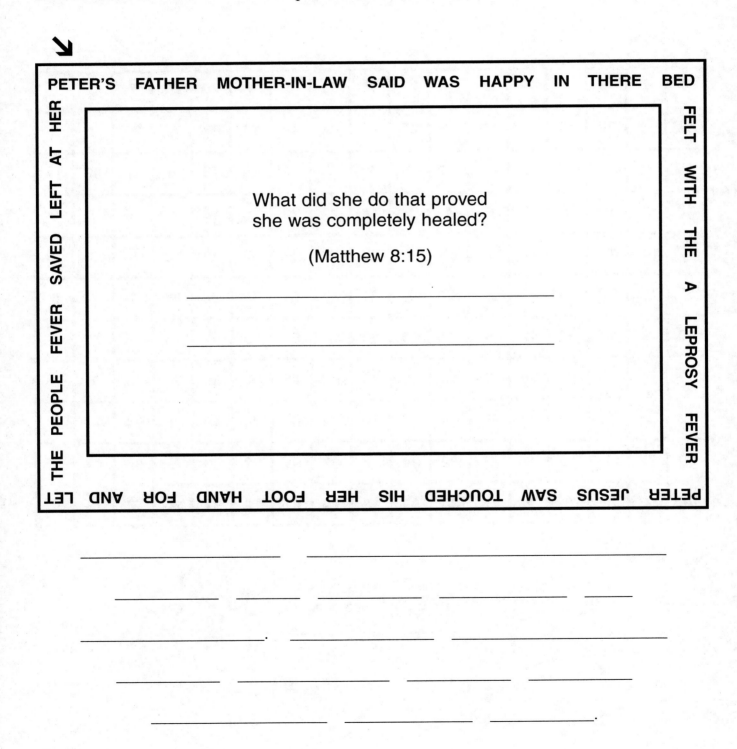

PETER'S   FATHER   MOTHER-IN-LAW   SAID   WAS   HAPPY   IN   THERE   BED

What did she do that proved
she was completely healed?

(Matthew 8:15)

_____

_____

Left side (bottom to top): HER AT LEFT SAVED FEVER PEOPLE THE

Right side (top to bottom): FELT WITH THE A LEPROSY FEVER

Bottom (right to left): PETER JESUS SAW TOUCHED HIS HER FOOT HAND FOR AND LET

_____   _____

_____   _____   _____   _____   _____   _____

_____   _____ . _____   _____   _____

_____   _____   _____   _____

_____   _____   _____ .

Jesus' Disciples

(Matthew 10:1–4)

Directions: Jesus had 12 disciples, hand-picked followers who traveled with Him, helping Him in His ministry and learning from Him how to serve God. See if you can find and circle all 12 of them in the word search puzzle. The leftover letters tell you who can be a disciple of Jesus. Write them in order on the lines below the puzzle.

If you need help, unscramble these names:

EEPRT

DEWRNA

ESMAJ

ONJH

LPIIPH

THOLBARMEWO

SHTOAM

ATTEHMW

MAJES

HDATEUSAD

NISOM

SDUJA

S	I	M	O	N	T	T	B
A	J	N	Y	O	H	H	A
P	N	O	E	W	A	O	R
H	E	O	H	S	D	M	T
L	O	T	E	N	D	A	H
V	E	M	E	S	A	S	O
J	A	N	D	R	E	W	L
J	A	M	E	S	U	E	O
S	J	U	D	A	S	U	M
P	H	I	L	I	P	S	E
♥	M	A	T	T	H	E	W

Who can be a disciple of Jesus?

___ ___ ___ ___ ___   ___ ___ ___

___ ___ ___ ___ ___   ___ ___ ___

A Demon-Possessed Man Is Healed

(Luke 8:26-39)

Jesus and His disciples met a demon-possessed man. Jesus healed him, making the demons come out of him and go into a herd of pigs instead. The man became a completely different person. He was so thankful, he wanted to go with Jesus.

Directions: What did Jesus tell the demon-possessed man to do instead? To find out, write the letter that comes between each pair of letters.

JESUS SAID,

"QS   DF   SU   TV   QS   MO   GI   NP   LN   DF

___ ___ ___ ___ ___ ___   ___ ___ ___ ___

ZB   MO   CE   SU   DF   KM   KM   GI   NP   VX

___ ___ ___   ___ ___ ___ ___   ___ ___ ___

LN   TV   BD   GI   FH   NP   CE   GI   ZB   RT

___ ___ ___ ___   ___ ___ ___   ___ ___ ___

CE   NP   MO   DF   EG   NP   QS   XZ   NP   TV."

___ ___ ___ ___   ___ ___ ___   ___ ___ ___

(Luke 8:39)

Jairus' Daughter

(Luke 8:40-42, 49-55)

Jairus came and asked Jesus to go home with him and heal his daughter who was dying. Jesus went with the man, but on the way someone came to tell Jairus that his daughter had died. Jesus went to the man's home and raised the girl from the dead.

Directions: Help Jairus and Jesus find their way through the maze to Jairus' daughter.

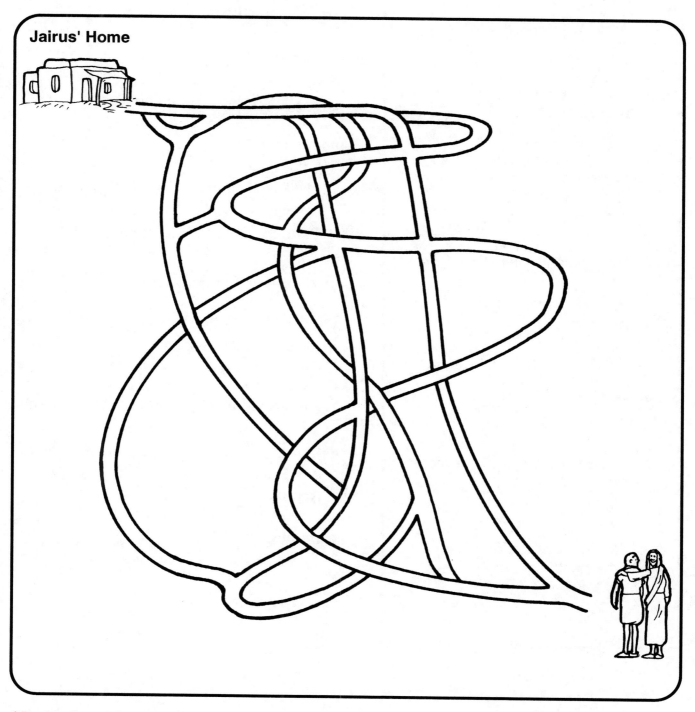

Jairus' Home

The Parable of the Sower

(Matthew 13:1–23)

Directions: Jesus told a parable (story) about a sower (farmer) who sowed (planted) some seeds. Complete the clues; then use your answers to complete the story.

CLUES

1. A trail to walk along

   _____

2. The parts of plants that are underground

   _____

3. Flying creatures such as sparrows

   _____

4. Prickly plants with sharp points

   _____

5. Opposite of bad

   _____

6. Stony

   _____

7. The shiny thing in the daytime sky

   _____

8. Flowers, bushes, and other growing things

   _____

A farmer planted some seeds. Some of them

fell along the _____ and the

_____ soon came and ate them.

Some seeds fell on _____

soil. The seeds came up but quickly died

when the _____ came up because

the _____ were too small.

Some seeds fell in soil where there were many

_____. The seeds

started to grow but were soon crowded out by

the larger _____. Some

seeds fell on _____ soil and

grew into big, healthy _____.

The Parable of the Lost Son

(Luke 15:11-32)

Jesus often told parables (stories) to teach important lessons. To explain how much God loves us, He told about a man with two sons. One son left home and lived foolishly. When he ran out of money, he decided to come home. How did his father feel about him coming home?

Directions: To find out what the father did, use the number/letter code to decode the Bible verse.

	CODE											
A	**B**	**C**	**D**	**E**	**F**	**G**	**H**	**I**	**J**	**K**	**L**	**M**
3	6	9	12	15	18	21	24	2	4	8	10	14
N	**O**	**P**	**Q**	**R**	**S**	**T**	**U**	**V**	**W**	**X**	**Y**	**Z**
16	20	22	26	1	5	7	11	13	17	19	23	25

$\overline{24}\ \overline{15}\quad \overline{1}\ \overline{3}\ \overline{16}\quad \overline{7}\ \overline{20}\quad \overline{24}\ \overline{2}\ \overline{5}\quad \overline{5}\ \overline{20}\ \overline{16}$,

$\overline{7}\ \overline{24}\ \overline{1}\ \overline{15}\ \overline{17}\quad \overline{24}\ \overline{2}\ \overline{5}\quad \overline{3}\ \overline{1}\ \overline{14}\ \overline{5}$

$\overline{3}\ \overline{1}\ \overline{20}\ \overline{11}\ \overline{16}\ \overline{12}\quad \overline{24}\ \overline{2}\ \overline{14}$, $\overline{3}\ \overline{16}\ \overline{12}$

$\overline{8}\ \overline{2}\ \overline{5}\ \overline{5}\ \overline{15}\ \overline{12}\quad \overline{24}\ \overline{2}\ \overline{14}$. (Luke 15:20b)

Five Thousand People Fed

(John 6:1-14)

Directions: Play the game to find out more about this story. Use a coin for a marker. Begin by moving one square forward. If the statement on the square you land on is *true*, go ahead *two squares*. If it is *false*, go ahead only *one square*. Continue this way around the squares until you reach the end.

START

Great crowds followed Jesus to see miracles. **1** (John 6:2)	Jesus took His disciples to a nearby town. **2** (John 6:3)	Jesus told Philip to send the people home. **3** (John 6:5)	Philip said they could not afford to feed them all. **4** (John 6:7)

Andrew said he had enough to feed them.

5

(John 6:8–9)

Jesus thanked God for the 5 loaves and 2 fish. **9** (John 6:11)	The people stayed standing. **8** (John 6:10)	The boy had 5 fish and 2 small bread loaves. **7** (John 6:9)	Andrew found a boy who would share his lunch. **6** (John 6:8–9)

There were about 1,000 people there that day.

10

(John 6:10)

There was enough to feed all 5,000 people. **11** (John 6:11)	They threw away the leftovers. **12** (John 6:12)	The disciples gathered 12 baskets of leftovers. **13** (John 6:13)	Everyone thought Jesus was a Prophet. **14** (John 6:14)

END

Peter Walks on Water

(Matthew 14:22–33)

Directions: Number the pictures from 1 to 6 to show the order in which they happened.

_____ The disciples saw Jesus walking toward them on the water.

_____ Peter got out of the boat and walked on the water toward Jesus.

_____ Jesus reached out his hand and grabbed Peter. "Why did you doubt?" Jesus asked.

_____ Jesus' disciples were in a boat on the lake being tossed around by heavy winds.

_____ Suddenly, Peter looked around at the wind-tossed waves and began to sink.

_____ Jesus and Peter got into the boat and right away the wind calmed down.

(Luke 17:11-19)

Directions: Jesus healed ten men of their leprosy. To find out what only one of them did, get rid of the leprosy in each word by crossing out the letters LEPROSY, working left to right, in each box. Write the words that are left on the numbered lines.

LECPARMOSEY

1. _____

LEBPAROCSKY

4. _____

LTEHPARNOKSEYD

2. _____

LEGPORODSY

5. _____

LPERAPIRSOINSGY

3. _____

TLHERPERWOSY

6. _____

LEJPERSOUSSY

7. _____

When he saw he was healed, he

___ ___ ___ ___   ___ ___ ___ ___,
   1   4

___ ___ ___ ___ ___   ___ ___ ___ in a loud voice.
   3   5

He ___ ___ ___ ___ ___ himself at ___ ___ ___ ___ ___,
      6   7

feet and ___ ___ ___ ___ ___ ___ ___ him.
            2

(Luke 17:15-16)

The Good Shepherd
(John 10)

Jesus called Himself our Good Shepherd, and we are His sheep. To find out what the Shepherd did for us, follow the directions.

Directions: In the word pairs below, find the letter in one word that is not in the other word. Write them on the lines with the matching numbers to complete the Bible verse.

1. I am in CLACK but not in CLICK. _____

2. I am in DONE but not in ONE. _____

3. See me in SEAL but not in SAIL. _____

4. Look for me in FULL but not in PULL. _____

5. I am in GONE but not in DONE. _____

6. I appear in CHAP but not in CLAP. _____

7. Here I am in STILL but not in STALL. _____

8. I am in LOOSE but not in GOOSE. _____

9. See me in MANE but not in MADE. _____

10. I am in POST but not in PAST. _____

11. Find me in PAIL but not in MAIL. _____

12. I am in HARM but not in HAM. _____

13. Look for me in FAST but not in FAT. _____

14. See me in TORN but not in WORN. _____

15. I am in WASTE but not in HASTE. _____

16. See me in ROCKY but not in ROCK. _____

___ ___ ___   ___ ___ ___ ___   ___ ___ ___ ___ ___ ___ ___ ___
14 6   3   5 10 10   2   13 6   3 11 6   3 12   2

___ ___ ___ ___   ___ ___ ___ ___   ___ ___ ___
 8   1 16 13   2 10 15   9   6   7 13

___ ___ ___ ___   ___ ___ ___   ___ ___ ___
 8   7   4   3   4 10 12   14 6   3

___ ___ ___ ___ ___. (John 10:11)
13 6   3   3 11

Lazarus Is Raised from the Dead

(John 11:1–44)

Directions: Lazarus' sisters sent a message to Jesus that their brother was very sick. By the time Jesus arrived at their home, Lazarus had been dead and in his tomb for four days. That was no problem for Jesus. Use the phone code to discover an important call Jesus made and how it was answered. (Examples: -2 = A, 2 = B, 2- = C)

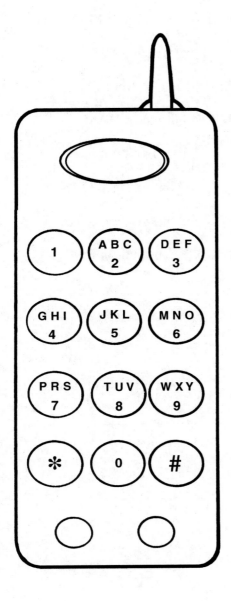

Jesus called in a loud voice, "Lazarus,

___ ___ ___ ___   ___ ___ ___!" The
2- 6- -6   3   6-   8 -8

___ ___ ___ ___   ___ ___ ___
-3   3 -2 -3   -6 -2   6

___ ___ ___ ___   ___ ___ ___, his
2- -2 -6   3   6-   8 -8

___ ___ ___ ___ ___ and
4   -2   6 -3 7-

___ ___ ___ ___ wrapped with strips of
3-   3   3 -8

linen, and a cloth around his

___ ___ ___ ___. (John 11:43–44)
3- -2 2-   3

Zacchaeus

(Luke 19:1-10)

Directions: Answer the questions to write a summary of this familiar story, then complete the Bible verse. Use the words in the word box.

```
                           WORD BOX

    Zacchaeus    seek      Pharisees    tree      miracle    Jerusalem

    disciples    Jesus     Jericho      river     lost       John

    healing      Son       boat         man       save       salvation
```

STORY SUMMARY

1. Who is this story about?

_____ and _____

2. Where did it happen?

In a _____ in _____

3. What happened?

_____

"The _____ of _____ came to

_____ and

_____ the _____." (Luke 19:10)

Jesus' Transfiguration

(Matthew 17:1-13)

Directions: Help Jesus and three of His disciples find their way up the mountain for His Transfiguration. Follow the letters that spell out the names of the two men who appeared with Him.

_____ and _____

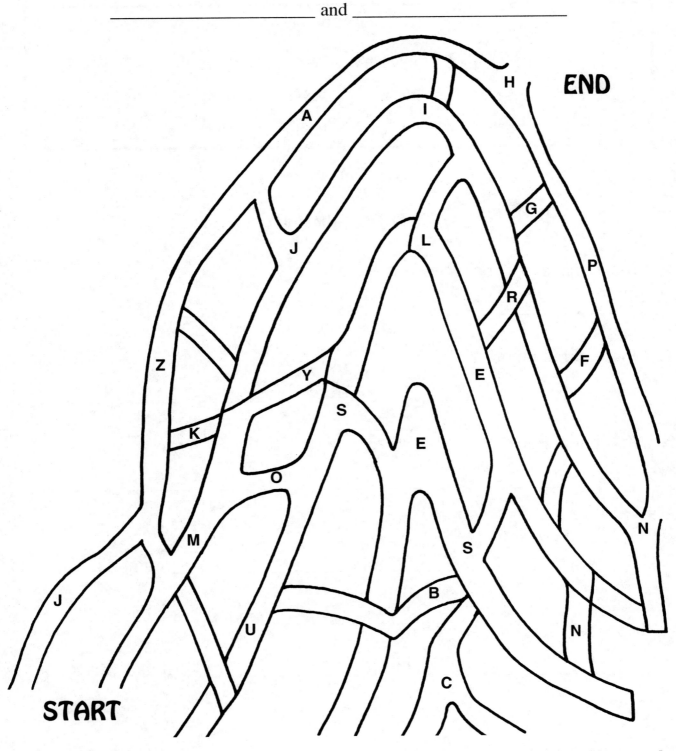

The Unmerciful Servant

(Matthew 18:21-35)

Directions: Jesus told a story about a king who showed mercy to a servant and canceled the debt he owed. That same servant then went out and had someone who owed him money put in prison. This made the king very angry. What was Jesus teaching with this story? To find out, cross out every square that contains double letters. Write the remaining letters on the lines.

EE	F	LL	O	SS	OO	R	G
I	MM	II	V	E	XX	O	T
YY	H	E	AA	R	OO	S	A
S	TT	G	BB	O	D	CC	ZZ
H	PP	A	EE	S	F	DD	O
RR	R	G	SS	I	V	II	E
N	LL	HH	Y	UU	BB	O	U

___ ___ ___ ___ ___ ___ ___   ___ ___ ___ ___ ___ ___

___ ___   ___ ___ ___   ___ ___ ___

___ ___ ___ ___ ___ ___ ___ ___   ___ ___ ___.

The Good Samaritan

(Luke 10:25-37)

An expert in the Law asked Jesus a question. To answer, Jesus told a story about a Samaritan who helped a man who had been robbed and beaten and left on the roadside. Two religious leaders passed him by without offering any help. To find out what question was asked and what Jesus was teaching with this story, follow the directions.

Directions: Write the letter that comes <u>after</u> each one given below.

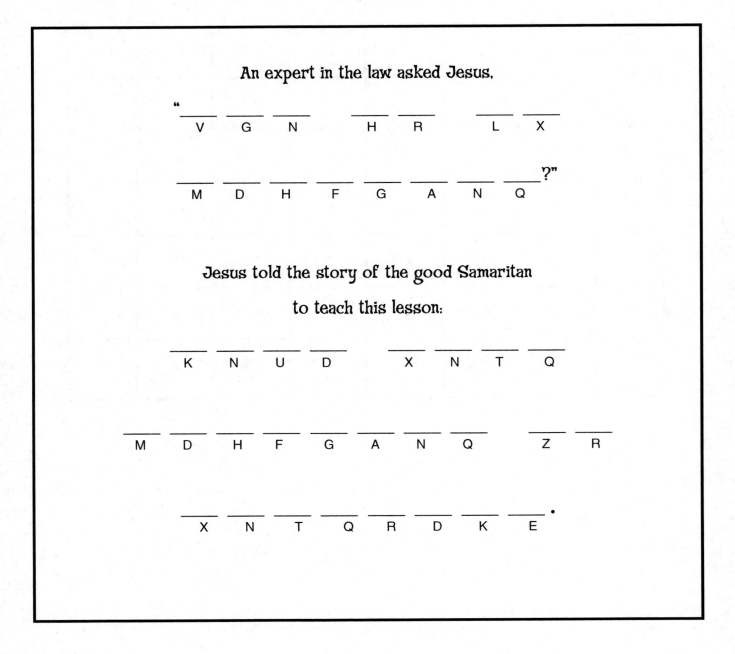

An expert in the law asked Jesus,

" ___ ___ ___   ___ ___   ___ ___
V G N   H R   L X

___ ___ ___ ___ ___ ___ ___ ___?"
M D H F G A N Q

Jesus told the story of the good Samaritan

to teach this lesson:

___ ___ ___ ___   ___ ___ ___ ___
K N U D   X N T Q

___ ___ ___ ___ ___ ___ ___ ___   ___ ___
M D H F G A N Q   Z R

___ ___ ___ ___ ___ ___ ___ ___ ___.
X N T Q R D K E

The Triumphal Entry

(Matthew 21:1-11)

Jesus knew some men in Jerusalem were plotting to kill Him, but he did not sneak into the city so no one would see Him. He rode in on a donkey with crowds of cheering people lined up along the street. He entered the city like a king even though He knew in a week He would die.

Directions: Complete the crossword puzzle with the words people shouted as Jesus rode by. **A** words go across; **D** words go down.

As Jesus rode by the people shouted, "**4-A** to the **7-D** of **8-D!**

5-A is **4-D 1-D 2-D** in the **3-D** of the **6-D!**" (Matthew 21:9)

Directions: Some of these words are ones we do not use much anymore. Write what you would shout if Jesus rode down your street today.

_____

_____

The Parable of the Talents

(Matthew 25:14–30)

Directions: Jesus told a story of a man who gave his servants some "talents" of money before he left on a trip. (One "talent" was worth about $1,000.) What did they do with all that money? Use the number code to complete the story.

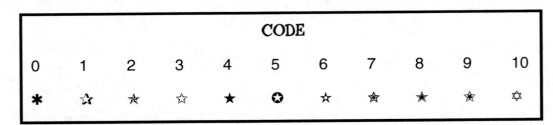

The first servant received _____ talents, or $_____ from his master. He doubled his

money: _____ talents x _____ = $_____.

The second servant received _____ talents, or $_____. He also doubled his

money: _____ talents x _____ = $_____.

The third servant received _____ talent, or $_____. Instead of trying to

invest the money wisely like the other servants did, he buried it in a hole in the ground.

_____ talent x _____ = $_____. He still had the $_____

he started out with, but that was all.

When the master returned, he was very pleased with the first servant who had

$_____ for him and with the second servant who had

$_____ for him. He was angry with the third servant. He took away his

$_____ and gave it to the first servant.

The Last Supper

(Mark 14:12-26)

Directions: The last meal Jesus had with His disciples before His death was to celebrate a Jewish holiday. Begin at the arrow; count four letters over. Write the fourth letter on the first line inside the box. Keep counting and writing down every fourth letter. You will discover the Jewish holiday Jesus and His disciples were celebrating.

↘

R	A	Q	P	L	M	Z	A	B	M	A	S
R											N
H											C
T				_ _ _ _ _ _ _ _						L
S											S
E	N	U	P	V	O	G	G	O	C	D	L

Jesus in the Garden

(Matthew 26:36-56)

Directions: When Jesus and His disciples finished their Passover meal, they went to a garden to pray. He left the other disciples and took Peter, James, and John a little farther away. Then he walked away by Himself to pray, knowing that He would be arrested and put to death that night. Shortly after Jesus finished praying, Judas came into the garden with a crowd of men armed with swords and clubs. They arrested Jesus and took Him away to be tried by Jewish religious leaders. What did Jesus pray in the garden? To find out, use the number/letter code box to complete the Bible verse.

	6	7	8	9
1	A	B	C	E
2	F	H	I	K
3	L	M	N	O
4	P	R	S	T
5	U	V	W	Y

$\overline{3\text{-}7}$ $\overline{5\text{-}9}$ $\overline{2\text{-}6}$ $\overline{1\text{-}6}$ $\overline{4\text{-}9}$ $\overline{2\text{-}7}$ $\overline{1\text{-}9}$ $\overline{4\text{-}7}$, $\overline{2\text{-}8}$ $\overline{2\text{-}6}$ $\overline{2\text{-}8}$ $\overline{4\text{-}9}$

$\overline{2\text{-}8}$ $\overline{4\text{-}8}$ $\overline{4\text{-}6}$ $\overline{3\text{-}9}$ $\overline{4\text{-}8}$ $\overline{4\text{-}8}$ $\overline{2\text{-}8}$ $\overline{1\text{-}7}$ $\overline{3\text{-}6}$ $\overline{1\text{-}9}$, $\overline{3\text{-}7}$ $\overline{1\text{-}6}$ $\overline{5\text{-}9}$

$\overline{4\text{-}9}$ $\overline{2\text{-}7}$ $\overline{2\text{-}8}$ $\overline{4\text{-}8}$ $\overline{1\text{-}8}$ $\overline{5\text{-}6}$ $\overline{4\text{-}6}$ $\overline{1\text{-}7}$ $\overline{1\text{-}9}$

$\overline{4\text{-}9}$ $\overline{1\text{-}6}$ $\overline{2\text{-}9}$ $\overline{1\text{-}9}$ $\overline{3\text{-}8}$ $\overline{2\text{-}6}$ $\overline{4\text{-}7}$ $\overline{3\text{-}9}$ $\overline{3\text{-}7}$ $\overline{3\text{-}7}$ $\overline{1\text{-}9}$.

$\overline{5\text{-}9}$ $\overline{1\text{-}9}$ $\overline{4\text{-}9}$ $\overline{3\text{-}8}$ $\overline{3\text{-}9}$ $\overline{4\text{-}9}$ $\overline{1\text{-}6}$ $\overline{4\text{-}8}$ $\overline{2\text{-}8}$ $\overline{5\text{-}8}$ $\overline{2\text{-}8}$ $\overline{3\text{-}6}$ $\overline{3\text{-}6}$,

$\overline{1\text{-}7}$ $\overline{5\text{-}6}$ $\overline{4\text{-}9}$ $\overline{1\text{-}6}$ $\overline{4\text{-}8}$ $\overline{5\text{-}9}$ $\overline{3\text{-}9}$ $\overline{5\text{-}6}$ $\overline{5\text{-}8}$ $\overline{2\text{-}8}$ $\overline{3\text{-}6}$ $\overline{3\text{-}6}$.

(Matthew 26:39)

Peter Denies Jesus

(Luke 22:54-62)

Directions: At their last supper together Jesus said that Peter would deny Him. Peter was shocked. He vowed that he would die for Jesus! But that same night Peter did exactly what Jesus said he would do. Solve the math problems to decode the words that complete the story.

```
                              CODE

    A      B      D      E      G      H      I      K      L      M
    7      13     5      10     8      4      12     6      9      15

           N      O      P      R      S      T      U      W      Y
           1      11     19     17     2      16     14     18     3
```

Peter waited in the courtyard while the high priest questioned Jesus. A servant girl

looked at Peter and said, "This man was with him."

Peter said, "___ ___ ___ ___ ___,   ___   ___ ___ ___ ___,
              9+9 8+3 10+5 12–5 7–6   9+3   12–7 9+2 3–2 19–3

___ ___ ___ ___   ___ ___ ___."
4+2 11–10 5+6 11+7   9–5 2+10 19–4

A little later someone else said, "You are one of them."

Peter replied, "___ ___ ___,   ___   ___ ___   ___ ___ ___!"
                9+6 10–3 3–2   13–1   5+2 11+4   12–11 3+8 13+3

An hour later a man pointed at Peter and said, "Certainly this fellow was with him."

"___ ___ ___,   ___   ___ ___ ___ ___   ___ ___ ___ ___
 12+3 13–6 1+0   6+6   10–5 19–8 13–12 13+3   2+4 4–3 15–4 12+6

___ ___ ___ ___   ___ ___ ___   ___ ___ ___,
25–7 2+2 11–4 19–3   12–9 30–19 5+9   5+12 19–9

___ ___ ___ ___ ___ ___ ___   ___ ___ ___ ___ ___!"
7+9 19–12 11–2 14–8 20–8 7–6 13–5   6+1 5+8 22–11 7+7 5+11

What did Peter do next?

___ ___   ___ ___ ___ ___   ___ ___ ___ ___ ___ ___ ___ ___.
12–8 8+2   11+7 14–4 17+2 3+13   24–11 4+8 12+4 20–4 8+2 14+3 14–5 11–8

Directions: Jesus was tried and found guilty by the Jewish leaders who wanted to get rid of Him. He was sent to Pilate to be sentenced to death. Then Roman soldiers took him to a hill outside the town to be crucified. When they got to the hill, He was hung on a cross to die. What did Jesus say before He died? Decode His last words below.

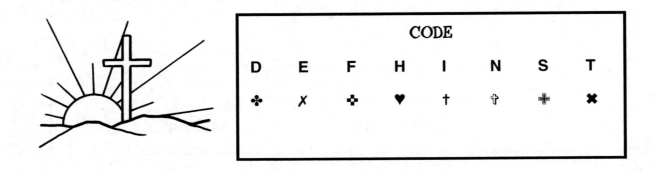

CODE

D	E	F	H	I	N	S	T

Jesus said,

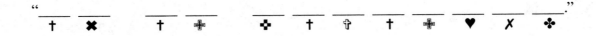

"IT IS FINISHED."

What did Jesus mean by those words?

(Look up Isaiah 53:5 and Romans 5:8 if you need help.)

The Resurrection

(Matthew 28:1-15)

Directions: Jesus died, but He did not stay dead. His Resurrection is a day all Christians everywhere celebrate with joy! Complete the Resurrection acrostic with the words you add to the story.

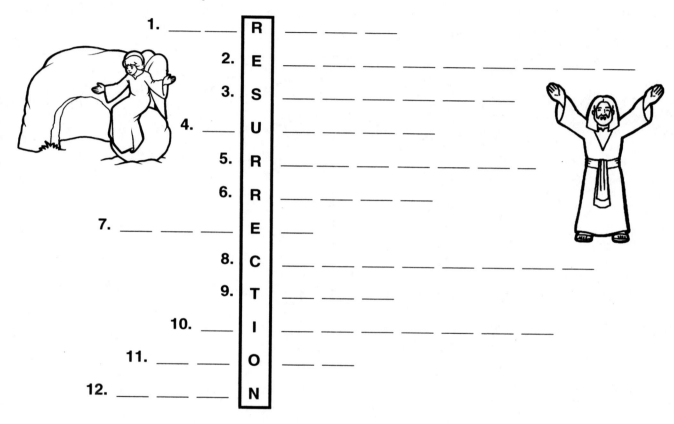

1. ___ ___ **R** ___ ___ ___
2.   **E** ___ ___ ___ ___ ___ ___ ___ ___
3.   **S** ___ ___ ___ ___ ___ ___
4.   **U** ___ ___ ___ ___ ___
5.   **R** ___ ___ ___ ___ ___ ___
6.   **R** ___ ___ ___ ___
7. ___ ___ ___ **E** ___ ___
8.   **C** ___ ___ ___ ___ ___
9.   **T** ___ ___ ___
10. ___ **I** ___ ___ ___ ___ ___ ___
11. ___ ___ **O** ___ ___
12. ___ ___ ___ **N**

After the __3__ was over, some of Jesus' women friends came at __12__ to visit Jesus' __9__. There had been a violent __2__ and an __7__ had rolled the __11__ away from the door. The __4__ assigned to keep anyone from breaking into the __9__ shook with fear when they saw the __7__. They ran away as fast as they could go! When the women arrived, they were met by the __7__ who said to them, "Don't be __1__. I know you are looking for Jesus who was __8__, but He is not here. He has __6__ from the dead just as He said. Come and see the place where He lay. Then go quickly and tell His __10__!" The women joyfully ran off to find the __10__. Meanwhile, the frightened __4__ went to the chief priests and __5__ what had happened. They were given money to say that Jesus' __10__ had stolen His body while the __4__ were asleep. The chief priests did not want anyone to know about Jesus' resurrection.

Jesus Goes Back to Heaven

(Acts 1:1-11)

Directions: Jesus and His disciples went to the Mount of Olives outside the city. He had risen from the dead 40 days earlier. Now it was time for Him to go back to heaven and leave His disciples and other followers to continue His work of helping people know God. What was His final message for His disciples? To find out, choose words from the wheel to complete the Bible verse below.

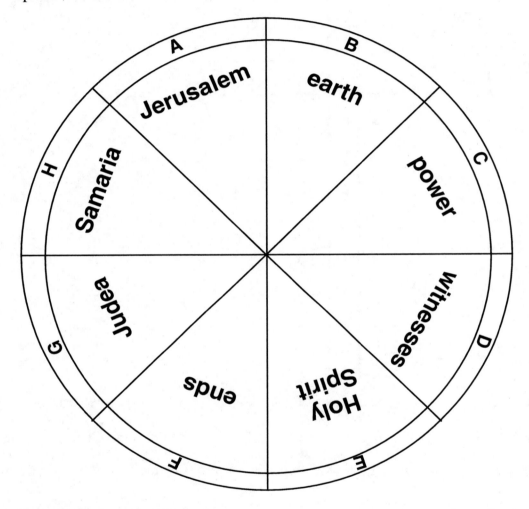

Jesus said, "You will receive _____ when the

C

_____ _____ comes on you; and you will be my

E

_____ in _____, and in all

D   A

_____ and _____ and to the

G   H

_____ of the _____." (Acts 1:8)

F   B

The Coming of the Holy Spirit

(Acts 2)

Before He went back to heaven, Jesus promised to send the Holy Spirit to help His followers be witnesses for Him. When the Holy Spirit came, He filled Jesus' followers and gave them the ability to speak in other languages so visitors from other lands could understand them. Many people gathered around to see what was happening. Peter preached about Jesus. To find out how many people believed in Jesus that day, follow the directions.

Directions: Connect all the even numbers in the box in order from the smallest to the largest. The last number you connect is the answer.

2	3	6	12	15	17	18	21
5	4	8	11	14	16	19	22
41	39	35	31	29	27	26	25
49	12	59	45	34	30	47	51
89	93	105	40	65	8	67	79
97	233	52	277	301	545	555	601
707	6	66	793	102	855	903	88
1035	88	100	1555	44	2001	2799	2
3333	224	500	4577	1000	90	5011	14
6575	48	7009	842	2044	20	8345	3000
8803	18	9015	122	9959	2222	2288	9999

The Early Church

(Acts 2:42-47)

Directions: How different was the New Testament church from our churches today? Unscramble the words (the numbers will help you) to complete the list of activities that were a part of the New Testament church. Then write the activities your church has to compare the two.

NEW TESTAMENT CHURCH	MY CHURCH

They devoted themselves to:

1. O S T A L E P S' _____
   3 4 5 1 6 7 2 8

   G H C T E A I N _____
   8 5 4 1 2 3 6 7

   and to

2. L O W S H F E L I P
   4 5 6 7 8 1 2 3 9 10

   _____, to the

3. B K R I E N A G   of   A D E R B
   1 5 2 6 3 7 4 8   4 5 3 2 1

   _____ of _____ and to

4. R A Y P E R   _____.
   2 3 4 1 5 6

5. They met Y R V E E _____
              5 4 2 3 1

   D Y A _____.
   1 3 2

6. They R I S D E P A _____
         2 4 5 7 6 1 3

   D G O _____.
   3 1 2

Peter and John at the Temple

(Acts 3)

Peter and John met a crippled beggar at the temple. Peter healed him and when people saw the healed man they crowded around and Peter talked to them about Jesus. What did the healed man do that attracted a crowd? To find out, follow the directions.

Directions: Cross out the following words in the boxes: words with double letters, words that begin with **R**, and words that end with **L**. Write the remaining words in order on the lines.

ATTRACT	HE	WILL	WENT	CALL	RENEW
WITH	RUNNING	THEM	INTO	COMMIT	THE
TEMPLE	UNTIL	RARE	COURTS	WALKING	ALL
MISS	AND	TOO	POOL	JUMPING	AND
REACHING	FEEL	PRAISING	RESISTING	NEED	GOD

__ __ __ __ __ __ __ __ __ __ __ __

__ __ __ __ __ __ __ __ __ __

__ __ __ __ __ __, __ __ __ __ __ __ __

__ __ __ __ __ __ __ __ __ __, __ __ __

__ __ __ __ __ __ __ __ __ __ __. (Acts 3:8)

Ananias and Sapphira

(Acts 5:1-11)

Directions: Solve the clues; then use the clue words to complete the story of Ananias and Sapphira.

CLUES

1. The parts of your body you walk on.

2. Coins and cash

3. Land that a person owns

4. Opposite of "lived"

5. Where you go for Sunday School

6. Third person of the Trinity

7. The woman in a marriage

8. Made a false statement

9. The man in a marriage

10. Fright

Ananias sold a piece of _____. He gave the _____ to the
                            3   2

_____, but kept back part of it for himself. His _____ Sapphira
         5   7

knew and approved of his actions. When he laid his gift at the apostles' _____,
                                                                                    1

Peter asked him, "Why have you _____ to the _____ _____
                                        8   6

and kept part of the _____ for yourself? You did not have to give any of it!" Suddenly,
                            2

Ananias fell down and _____. Some men carried his body away. Later, Sapphira came
                              4

in. She did not know what had happened to her _____. Peter asked her about
                                                          9

the price Ananias had received for their _____. Sapphira also _____.
                                                  3   8

When Peter told her about Ananias' death, suddenly, she fell down and _____, too!
                                                                                4

Great _____ filled all those who heard about Ananias and Sapphira.
            10

Christians Are Persecuted

(Acts 5:17-42)

Many of the Jewish religious leaders were jealous of the attention that was directed toward Jesus' disciples. They performed miracles, healing people and telling them about Jesus. More and more people believed in Jesus and joined the church. The religious leaders had some of the disciples arrested and put in jail, but during the night an angel released them! The disciples did not run and hide so they would not be arrested again. No, they went right back and preached in the temple courts.

Directions: Choose the correct ending for each word to tell what happened next.

```
WORD ENDINGS

        ict        ey        me        st

   od          ers        ch        est        en
```

The high pri_____ said, "We gave you str_____

ord_____ not to tea_____ in this na_____."

Peter and the others replied, "We mu_____ ob_____

G_____ rather than m_____!" (Acts 5:28-29)

Persecution of Christians did not stop; in fact, it got worse. Christians are still being persecuted in many places today. Why do you think people have such bad feelings toward Christians?

_____

_____

Stephen Is Killed

(Acts 6:8–7:60)

Stephen is called the first martyr of the church. That means he was the first Christian to be killed for his faith in Jesus. Stephen was a godly man, but he had enemies who wanted to get rid of him. They had him falsely accused and tried. He was found guilty of something he had not done and sentenced to death. The people threw stones at him until they killed him. To find out why his enemies wanted to have him killed and what Stephen's last words were, follow the directions.

Directions: In the sentences below, change every:

| V to O |
| F to E |
| Z to D |
| Q to I |

Why did Stephen's enemies want to get rid of him?

THFY   CVULZ   NVT   STANZ   UP   AGAQNST   HQS

_____

WQSZVM   VR   THF   SPQRQT   BY   WHVM   HF   SPVKF.

_____

What were the last words Stephen said as he was dying?

LVRZ,   ZV   NVT   HVLZ   THQS   SQN   AGAQNST   THFM.

_____

Philip and the Ethiopian

(Acts 8:26–39)

An angel told Philip to go down a certain road, but did not state why. He obeyed and met a man who needed his help. God used Philip to lead the man to receive Jesus as His Savior.

Directions: Complete the summary of the story by writing the letter that comes between the two letters given.

STORY SUMMARY

1. Who is in this story?

_____ _____ _____ _____ _____ _____
O Q   G I   H J   K M   H J   O Q

_____ _____ _____ _____ _____ _____ _____ _____ _____
D F   S U   G I   H J   N P   O Q   H J   Z B   M O

2. Where does the story take place?

In a ___ ___ ___ ___ ___ ___ ___ on the
  B D G I Z B Q S H J N P S U

_____ _____ _____ _____   _____ _____   _____ _____ _____ _____
Q S   N P   Z B   C E   S U   N P   F H   Z B   Y A   Z B

3. What happened?

The man was ___ ___ ___ ___ ___ ___ ___.
       Q S D F Z B C E H J M O F H

The other man told him the ___ ___ ___ ___   ___ ___ ___ ___.
                    F H N P N P C E   M O D F V X R T

The man believed and was ___ ___ ___ ___ ___ ___ ___ ___.
                  A C Z B O Q S U H J Y A D F C E

Saul Meets Jesus

(Acts 9:1-19)

Directions: Saul was a man who persecuted Christians in Jerusalem. Then he decided to go to Damascus to bring Christians back to Jerusalem to put them in prison. But on his way to Damascus, something happened to Saul that changed his life forever and turned him from a persecutor into a preacher. Number the pictures from 1 to 6 to show the order in which they happened.

____ The men with Saul heard the sound, but didn't see anything or anyone.

____ Saul fell to the ground and heard a voice say, "Saul, why are you persecuting me?"

____ Saul asked who was speaking. It was Jesus. He told Saul to get up and go into the city.

____ God sent a man named Ananias to give Saul back his sight. Then he got up and was baptized.

____ Near Damascus, a light from heaven flashed around Saul.

____ Saul was blind when he got up and his companions had to lead him to the city.

Saul Starts Preaching

(Acts 9:20–31)

After Saul met Jesus, he did not waste any time. He started preaching right away. How did people react to the difference they saw and heard in Saul?

Directions: Complete the crossword puzzle with the words that are missing from the sentences below. Then unscramble the letters in the gray boxes to discover the name of the person who spoke up for Saul to the Christians. Write the name on the lines below. **A** words go across; **D** words go down.

Saul <u>1-D</u> the <u>6-D</u> living in Damascus by <u>5-D</u> that Jesus is the <u>2-D</u>. After many days

had gone by, the Jews plotted to <u>7-D</u> him. The <u>4-A</u> in Jerusalem were <u>3-A</u> of him,

not <u>8-A</u> that he really was a disciple.

A well-known Christian named ____ ____ ____ ____ ____ ____ ____ ____

spoke up for Saul and told the disciples that Saul was really a Christian now.

Dorcas Is Given Back Her Life

(Acts 9:36-42)

In the town of Joppa, Dorcas was a popular person because she was always doing good and helping the poor. When she became sick and died, everyone was very sad. The disciples sent for Peter. When he arrived, he went by himself into the room where Dorcas' body had been laid. Peter prayed, then he told Dorcas to get up. She opened her eyes, saw Peter, and sat up. He took her hand and helped her stand up, alive again!

Directions: What happened when people heard what had happened to Dorcas? To find out, starting at the arrow, print the **M**, then every other letter on the lines below. Stop when you get to the star.

↓

```
M S A R N E Y T P R E L O L P K L O E N B S
★                                           E
D                                           N
P                                           L
R                                           R
O                                           I
O T L M E S H Y T B N S I J D Z E W V K E O
```

When news of what happened to Dorcas got around,

___ ___ ___ ___   ___ ___ ___ ___ ___

___ ___ ___ ___ ___ ___

___ ___ ___   ___ ___ ___   ___ ___ ___ ___ ___.

Peter and Cornelius

(Acts 10)

God gave Cornelius, a godly Roman soldier, a vision. An angel told him to send for Peter. Right away Cornelius sent three men to Joppa to ask Peter to come to his house. Meanwhile, Peter was having a vision about clean and unclean animals. God used the vision to help Peter see that if God said something was pure, it couldn't be unclean.

Directions: Why was this a lesson Peter needed to learn at that time? Decode the words to find out.

CODE

A	C	E	G	H	I	J	L
✱	✛	★	✝	✪	✚	✿	✳

N	O	P	R	S	T	U	W
⊞	☎	✈	♠	▶	♥	✂	❀

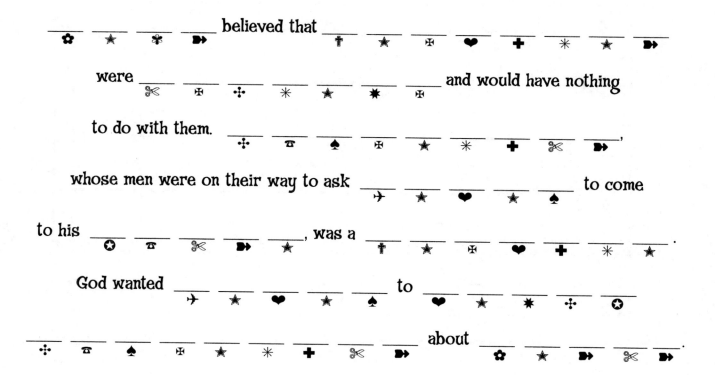

_____ believed that _____ were _____ and would have nothing to do with them. _____, whose men were on their way to ask _____ to come to his _____, was a _____. God wanted _____ to _____ _____ about _____.

Peter obeyed God and went to Cornelius' home. Cornelius and his whole family were saved.

Peter's Escape from Prison

(Acts 12:1-19)

Peter had been put in prison, but he did not stay there long. God sent an angel to help him escape from prison, much to the surprise of the friends who were praying for him! When Peter came to the house where the prayer meeting was taking place, they almost did not let him inside. They were sure it could not be him at the door.

Directions: Help Peter find his way through the maze to freedom. Then write the letters you passed over on the lines below to find out what this story teaches us.

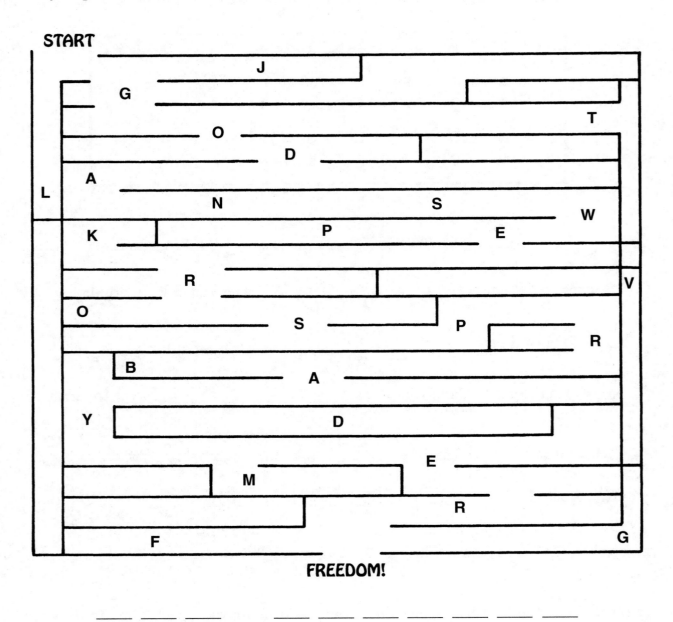

START

J   G   T   O   D   A   L   N   S   W   K   P   E   R   V   O   S   P   R   B   A   Y   D   E   M   R   F   G

FREEDOM!

___ ___ ___ ___   ___ ___ ___ ___

___ ___ ___ ___ ___ .

Paul's First Missionary Trip

(Acts 13-14)

Paul and Barnabas were led by the Holy Spirit to take a trip to Cyprus, then on to Lystra and Derbe and other places to spread the Gospel. When they got home, they reported to the church that God had saved many Gentiles. It was Paul's first missionary trip. Follow the directions to find out the town from which they left and to which they returned.

Directions: Color all the boxes that have only 1 dot in them. Then write the word in the blanks below that the colored boxes spell.

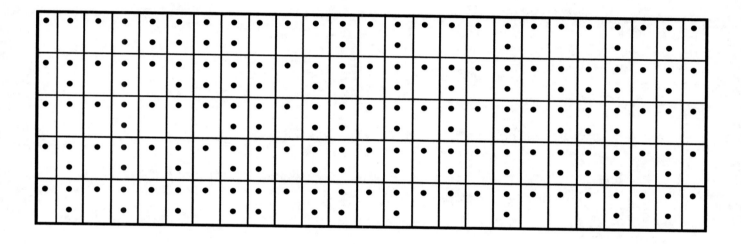

The church in the town of

____ ____ ____ ____ ____ ____ ____

sent Paul and Barnabas

out on this first missionary trip,

and they came back there at the end of the trip.

Paul and Silas Spread the Gospel

(Acts 15:40–16:15)

On his second missionary trip, Paul traveled with Silas. They visited some of the churches that had started as a result of Paul's first trip. When they got to the town of Lystra, they added a third man to their team. To find out his name and to discover one of the results of this second trip, follow the directions.

Directions: Cross out the double letters in each word below and write the new word on the line.

In Lystra, _____ joined
PPTLLIMIIOTEEHY

Paul and Silas on their missionary trip.

What were the results of this second trip?

The _____ were strengthened in the
CYYHUDDRCWWHES

_____ and _____
EEFALLITH   GLLRECCW

_____ in _____ .
BBDOOAILKKY   NTTUSSMBEHHRS

#7047 Bible Puzzles and Games   124   ©Teacher Created Resources, Inc.

Praising God in Prison

(Acts 16:16-40)

Directions: Complete this story of Paul and Silas by choosing the correct ending for each word from the box. Some word endings will be used more than once.

WORD ENDINGS

ed	uake	er	on	ying	ening	eve
ins	ippi	et	ging	en	ns	ors

In the city of Phil_____ Paul and Silas were beat_____ and then

thrown into pris_____. The jail_____ put their fe_____ in stocks to make

sure they did not escape. Late that night instead of complaining, Paul and Silas were

pra_____ and sin_____ hym_____ to God. The other prisoners

were list_____ to them. Suddenly, an earthq_____ shook the

pris_____ ! All the do_____ came open and everyone's cha_____

came loose. The jail_____ woke up and saw the open do_____. He

thought all the prisoners had escaped and he was going to kill himself. Then Paul

shouted to him, "We are all here!" The jail_____ rushed in and fell down before

Paul and Silas. "What must I do to be sav_____?" he asked them. They told him,

"Beli_____ in the Lord Jesus and you will be sav_____." That night the

jail_____ in Phil_____ became a Christian!

Paul Preaches in Athens

(Acts 17:15-34)

Sometimes Paul faced danger on his missionary trips. In Thessalonica some Jews who were jealous of Paul's success gathered a mob and started causing trouble. That night some Christians sent Paul and Silas to Berea, a nearby town. However, soon the troublemakers from Thessalonica found out where they were and came to Berea. Some friends took Paul to Athens, where he waited for Silas and Timothy. Paul preached a sermon in Athens, and many people responded by believing in Jesus.

Directions: Use the number code to decode what Paul said.

CODE											
A	B	C	D	E	G	H	I	J	K	L
1	7	8	9	2	10	11	3	12	13	14
M	N	O	R	S	T	U	V	W	Y	
15	16	4	17	18	19	5	20	21	6	

Paul said, "I found an __ __ __ __ __ inscribed to the
              1 14 19 1 17

__ __ __ __ __ __ __   __ __ __ .
5 16 13 16 4 21 16   10 4 9

I will tell you about this God.

The God who made the __ __ __ __ __ and
                      21 4 17 14 9

__ __ __ __ __ __ __ __ __ __ in it is the
2 20 2 17 6 19 11 3 16 10

__ __ __ __ of __ __ __ __ __ __ and
14 4 17 9   11 2 1 20 2 16

__ __ __ __ __ . In Him we __ __ __ __ and
2 1 17 19 11   14 3 20 2

__ __ __ __ and have our __ __ __ __ __ .
15 4 20 2   7 2 3 16 10

He will __ __ __ __ __ the world with
         12 5 9 10 2

__ __ __ __ __ __ __ by the __ __ __ He
12 5 18 19 3 8 2   15 1 16

has appointed."

What "man" do you think Paul was talking about? _____

A Fall from a Window

(Acts 20:6-12)

Directions: In the city of Troas on one of Paul's missionary trips, a strange thing happened. Paul was preaching in a crowded upstairs room late at night. By midnight, a young man sitting on a window ledge had fallen asleep. To find out what happened, write the numbered words on the lines with the matching numbers.

man 7	touched 13	ran 17	dead 4	you 16
saved 14	ground 2	put 20	upstairs 11	arms 8
alive 10	must 19	fell 1	alarmed 9	felt 15
third 3	Paul 5	ate 12	himself 6	began 18

He _____ to the _____ from the
         1   2

_____ story and was picked up _____ .
     3   4

_____ threw _____ on the young
     5   6

_____ and put his _____ around him. "Don't be
     7   8

_____ ," he said. "He's _____ !"
     9   10

Then he went _____ again
             11

and broke bread and _____ .
             12

Paul Is Arrested

(Acts 21:27-26:32)

Directions: Write the words on the lines to complete Paul's story; then find and circle the words in the word search puzzle.

GOD
QUESTIONED
SON
JERUSALEM
ARRESTED
ROME
CHAINS
TRIAL
KILL
COURAGE
CHURCH
RESCUED
GUARD
TWO
SISTER
CAESAREA

J	Q	U	E	S	T	I	O	N	E	D
S	E	Z	R	O	B	A	A	W	Y	T
F	T	R	V	N	S	R	R	O	M	E
Z	C	R	U	N	Q	G	R	S	S	C
G	H	G	I	S	M	O	E	T	S	A
C	H	A	L	A	A	D	S	W	I	E
P	H	D	K	I	L	L	T	O	S	S
C	O	U	R	A	G	E	E	N	T	A
A	B	A	R	Z	Q	G	D	M	E	R
J	R	E	S	C	U	E	D	V	R	E
G	U	A	R	D	H	P	L	N	B	A

Paul went to the city of _____. He received a warm welcome from the

_____, but not from some other people. An angry crowd grabbed him and tried

to _____ him. Roman soldiers _____ him, but then

_____ him. They put him in _____ and the next day took

him to be _____ by the Jewish religous leaders. That night God said to

Paul, "Take _____! You will testify about me in _____." More than

40 Jews plotted to kill Paul, but the _____ of his _____ heard about it and

told the Roman commander. He took Paul to _____ with hundreds

of soldiers to _____ him on the way. Paul stood _____ before

Governor Felix who then kept him around for _____ years. Finally, he was questioned by

King Agrippa who said Paul should be sent to Rome, just as _____ had said!

Shipwrecked!

(Acts 27:1-28:10)

Paul was a prisoner on his way to Rome on a ship with other prisoners. Suddenly, they were caught in a storm that was so bad, they tied ropes around the ship to try to keep it from breaking apart. The next day they threw the cargo overboard to lighten the ship; but nothing helped.

Directions: Choose words from the wheel to complete what Paul said to encourage everyone.

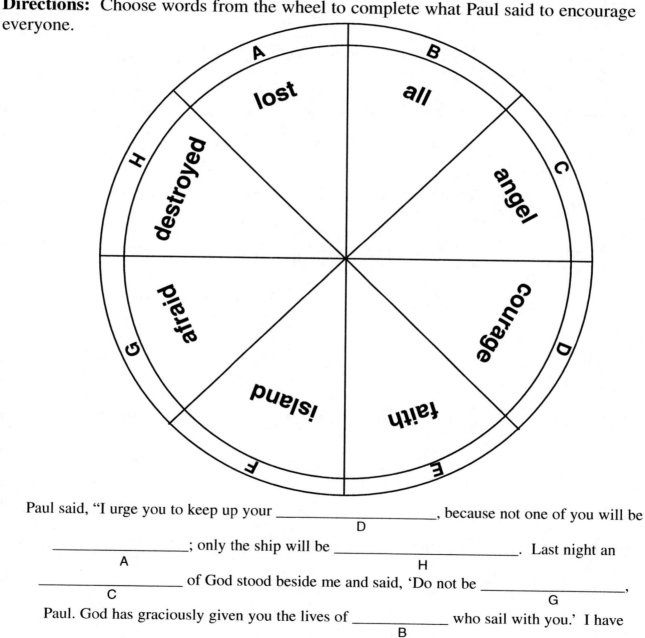

Paul said, "I urge you to keep up your _____, because not one of you will be

                                           D

_____; only the ship will be _____. Last night an

         A   H

_____ of God stood beside me and said, 'Do not be _____,

   C   G

Paul. God has graciously given you the lives of _____ who sail with you.' I have

                                                        B

_____ in God that it will happen just as He told me. We will run

   E

aground on some _____."

                        F

Philemon and Onesimus

(Philemon)

Onesimus was a slave who ran away from his master, Philemon. God worked it out that Onesimus met Paul in Rome. Paul talked to him about Jesus, and Onesimus believed and accepted Christ as his Savior. Then Paul sent him back to his master. Onesimus knew it was the right thing to do, but what would Philemon do to him? According to the law, a master could have a runaway slave killed. Paul wrote a letter to Philemon about his born-again slave.

Directions: To find out what Paul wrote about Onesimus, write the letter that comes between the two letters given in each word below.

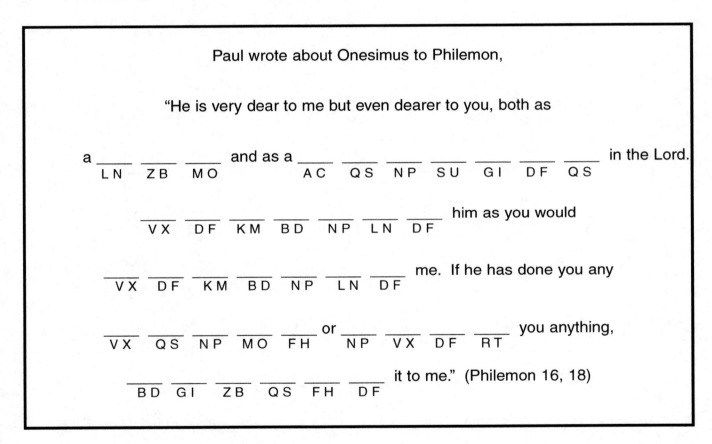

Paul wrote about Onesimus to Philemon,

"He is very dear to me but even dearer to you, both as

a ___ ___ ___ and as a ___ ___ ___ ___ ___ ___ ___ in the Lord.
  LN ZB MO   AC QS NP SU GI DF QS

___ ___ ___ ___ ___ ___ him as you would
VX DF KM BD NP LN DF

___ ___ ___ ___ ___ ___ me. If he has done you any
VX DF KM BD NP LN DF

___ ___ ___ ___ ___ or ___ ___ ___ ___ you anything,
VX QS NP MO FH   NP VX DF RT

___ ___ ___ ___ ___ ___ it to me." (Philemon 16, 18)
BD GI ZB QS FH DF

The Bible does not tell us what happened when Onesimus got home. What do you think Philemon did?

_____

_____

John's Vision of Heaven

(Revelation 21:1–22:5)

Directions: God gave John a vision of heaven, which he wrote about in the book of Revelation. Solve each clue. Then write the answer in the correct box to show what will be in heaven and what will not be in heaven.

CLUES

1. First word: another name for Jesus (sheep)
2. Second word: what you enjoy reading
3. Third word: Opposite of "death"
4. Opposite of "death"
5. A king's special chair
6. First word: roads in town
7. Second word: very precious metal
8. God's heavenly messengers
9. The One who created us
10. Opposite of "life"
11. Opposite of "day"
12. Another word for "weeping"
13. What shines in the daytime sky
14. The round object that shines in the nighttime sky
15. The building where Jews worshiped God
16. The feeling when something hurts
17. Things we turn on in the house at night for light

These will be in heaven.

Those whose names are written in the

_____ _____
　　1　　　　　　2

of _____,
　　　　　3

River of _____,
　　　　　　4

_____ of God,
　　5

_____ of _____,
　6　　　　　　　7

_____,
　　8

_____
　　9

These will not be in heaven.

_____,
　　10

_____,
　　11

_____,
　　12

_____,
　　13

_____,
　　14

_____,
　　15

_____,
　　16

_____
　　17

Page 6

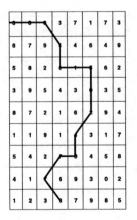

Page 7

When the woman saw that the fruit of the tree was good for food and pleasing to the eye, and also desirable for gaining wisdom, she took some and ate it.

She also gave some to her husband, who was with her, and he ate it.

Page 8

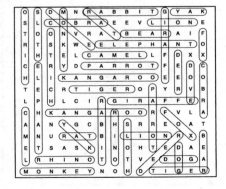

Page 9

Page 10

5. BUILDING
4. UNDERSTAND
3. BRICKS
2. EARTH
1. LANGUAGE

Page 11

Cross out the following words: cat, blue, two, purple, one, red, dog, four, pink, ten, yellow, lion, seven, three, five, bear, black.

Abraham was <u>100</u> years old.

Sarah was <u>90</u> years old.

Page 12

1. SERVANT
2. GOD
3. PRAYED
4. CAMELS
5. WORSHIPED
6. REBEKAH

Page 13

ESAU BECAME A SKILLFUL HUNTER, A MAN OF THE OPEN COUNTRY, WHILE JACOB WAS A QUIET MAN STAYING AMONG THE TENTS.

Page 14

1. LEAH
2. RACHEL
3. SEVEN
4. MARRIAGE
5. SEVEN
6. WIVES
7. RACHEL
8. TWELVE
9. JOSEPH
10. BENJAMIN

Page 15

1. BAD REPORT
2. LOVED
3. DREAMS
4. KILL
5. STRIPPED, ROBE

6. CISTERN
7. SOLD, EGYPT
8. GOAT, BLOOD
9. FATHER
10. ANIMAL

Answer Key

Page 16

THE LORD WAS WITH JOSEPH AND GAVE HIM SUCCESS IN WHATEVER HE DID.

Page 17

3, 5
6, 2
1, 4

Page 18

1. GO. I AM SENDING YOU
2. TO PHAROAH TO BRING
3. MY PEOPLE, THE ISRAELITES,
4. OUT OF EYGPT.

Page 19

1. blood
2. frogs
3. gnats
4. flies
5. death
6. boils
7. hail
8. locusts
9. darkness
10. death

Page 20

Page 22

The following commandments should be colored yellow: 1, 2, 3, 4.
The following commandments should be colored blue: 5, 6, 7, 8, 9, 10.

Page 23

1. Then
2. have
3. them
4. make
5. a
6. sanctuary
7. for
8. me
9. and
10. I
11. will
12. dwell
13. among
14. them

Page 24

1. BURNT OFFERING
2. GRAIN OFFERING
3. FELLOWSHIP OFFERING
4. SIN OFFERING
5. GUILT OFFERING

Page 25

1. rabbit
2. pig
3. trout
4. cow
5. bat
6. lizard
7. grasshopper
8. owl
9. clam
10. sheep

Page 26

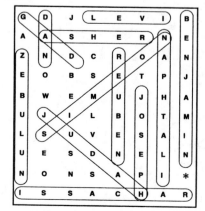

JACOB'S TWELVE SONS

Answer Key

Page 27

IF THE LORD IS PLEASED WITH US, HE WILL LEAD US INTO THAT LAND.

Page 28

ANGEL, SWORD, BOWED, ANGEL, PATH, DONKEY, AWAY, AWAY, YOU, SPARED

Page 29

"<u>BLESSED</u> are you, O Israel! Who is like you, a <u>PEOPLE</u> <u>SAVED</u> by the <u>LORD</u>?
He is your <u>SHIELD</u> and <u>HELPER</u> and your glorious <u>SWORD</u>. Your <u>ENEMIES</u> will cower before you and you will trample down their high places."

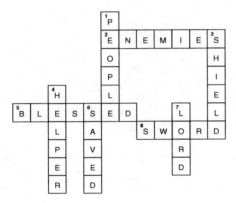

Page 30

CROSS THE JORDAN RIVER

Page 31

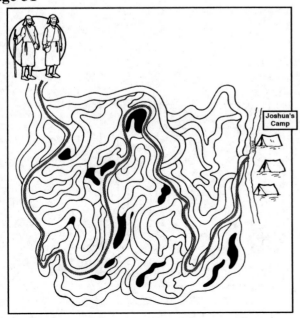

Page 32

a. 1
b. 6
c. 7
d. 7
e. 7
f. 6
g. 1
h. 1
i. 2
The Lord

Page 33

2, 4
5, 1
3, 6

Page 34

THE MEN OF ISRAEL SAMPLED THEIR PROVISIONS BUT DID NOT INQUIRE OF THE LORD.

Page 35

1 Across: EHUD
1 Down: EVIL
2 Across: JABIN
2 Down: BARAK
3 Across: SISERA
3 Down: ISRAEL
4 Across DEBORAH
4 Down: EPHRAIM

Page 36

Gideon's Army: 10000, 300
An Unusual Battle: TRUMPETS, TORCHES, JARS, TRUMPETS, JARS, SHOUTED

Page 37

1. C	A—LION
2. H	B—DELILAH
3. E	C—ANGEL
4. A	D—HAIR
5. F	E—PHILISTINES
6. B	F—DONKEY
7. G	G—STRENGTH
8. D	H—NAZIRITE
9. I	I—TEMPLE

Answer Key

Page 38

A—2
B—4
C—7
D—5

E—1
F—3
G—6

Bottom Answer: David

Page 39

Hannah told Eli, "I PRAYED for this CHILD and the LORD has granted me what I asked of him. So now I GIVE him to the LORD. For his WHOLE life he will be GIVEN over to the LORD."

Page 40

THE LORD WAS WITH SAMUEL AS HE GREW UP, AND ISRAEL RECOGNIZED THAT SAMUEL WAS A PROPHET OF THE LORD.

Page 41

God chose SAUL, an impressive YOUNG man without EQUAL among the Israelites—a HEAD TALLER than any of the OTHERS.

Page 42

NOTHING CAN HINDER THE LORD FROM SAVING, WHETHER BY MANY OR BY FEW.

Page 43

4, 3
6, 1
2, 5

Page 44

1. I killed a lion and bear to protect my sheep.
2. He has been a fighting man from his youth.
3. Goliath's weapons: bronze helmet, bronze leg armor, huge spear, shield, bronze javelin, bronze armor
   David's weapons: sling, five stones
4A. I
4B. COME
4C. AGAINST
4D. YOU
4E. IN
4F. NAME
4G. LORD
4H. ALMIGHTY

Page 45

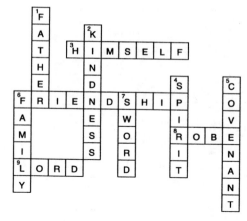

Page 46

Samuel said, "The Lord will HAND OVER BOTH ISRAEL AND YOU TO THE PHILISTINES, and tomorrow YOU and your SONS will be with me."

Page 47

1. attack
2. circle
3. quickly
4. straight
5. strike
6. marching
7. front
8. Lord
9. behind
10. trees

God told David, "Do not go STRAIGHT up, but CIRCLE around BEHIND them and ATTACK them in front of the balsam TREES. As soon as you hear the sound of MARCHING in the tops of the balsam TREES, move QUICKLY, because that will mean the LORD has gone out in FRONT of you to STRIKE the Philistine army.

Page 48

YOUR HOUSE AND YOUR KINGDOM WILL ENDURE FOREVER BEFORE ME; YOUR THRONE WILL BE ESTABLISHED FOREVER.

Page 49

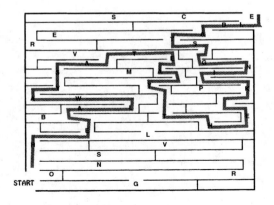

HE ALWAYS ATE AT THE KING'S TABLE.

Page 50

1. True	9. True
2. False	10. False
3. True	11. True
4. False	12. True
5. True	13. True
6. False	14. False
7. True	15. True
8. False	16. True

Page 51

AS ABSALOM'S MULE WENT UNDER THE THICK BRANCHES OF A LARGE OAK, HIS HEAD GOT CAUGHT IN THE TREE. HE WAS LEFT HANGING IN MIDAIR, WHILE THE MULE KEPT GOING. WHEN DAVID'S, GENERAL SAW ABSALOM HANGING THERE, HE KILLED HIM.

Page 52

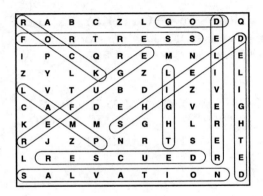

Page 53

1. G		8. M
2. S		9. E
3. A		10. K
4. D		11. T
5. W		12. P
6. L		13. R
7. O		14. N

David told Solomon, "Be STRONG, show yourself a MAN, and observe what the LORD your God requires: WALK in his ways, and KEEP his decrees and commands."

Page 54

Materials Used: C E D A R and P I N E from Lebanon, and G O L D

Workers: 3 0, 0 0 0 sent to Lebanon to help cut the wood; 7 0, 0 0 0 carriers; 8 0, 0 0 0 stone cutters, 3, 3 0 0 foremen to supervise the work

Temple Decorations: Solomon had A N G E L S, F L O W E R S, and P A L M   T R E E S carved on the walls and doors.

Time: It took 7 Y E A R S to complete the temple.

Page 55

1. SILVER	5. WISDOM
2. HORSES	6. CHARIOTS
3. PALACE	7. THRONE
4. GOLD	

Page 56

I WILL TEAR THE KINGDOM AWAY FROM YOU, NOT DURING YOUR LIFETIME BUT DURING YOUR SON'S.

Page 57

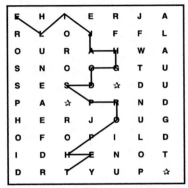

HER JAR OF FLOUR WAS NOT USED UP AND HER JUG OF OIL DID NOT DRY UP.

Page 58

    4, 6
    1, 5
    3, 2

Page 59

Main Characters: AHAB, NABOTH, JEZEBEL, ELIJAH
Places: PALACE, VINEYARD
Actions: CURSED, STONED
AHAB saw a VINEYARD he wanted for his own, but NABOTH, the owner, would not sell it. AHAB went home to his PALACE and pouted. When is wife, JEZEBEL, found out what was wrong, she promised to take care of it for him. She arranged for the leaders of the town where NABOTH lived to accuse him of blasphemy in front of the people. Two evil men falsely testified that NABOTH had CURSED God. Then he was STONED. AHAB happily went to take possession of his new property. But ELIJAH was there to meet him. He told the king that God was going to bring disaster on him and his family because of what he had done.

Page 60

Elijah went to heaven in a CHARIOT of FIRE pulled by HORSES of FIRE in a WHIRLWIND!

Page 61

    A. salt   1. B
    B. staff   2. A
    C. oil   3. E
    D. flour   4. C
    E. bread   5. D

Page 62

Elisha told Naaman, "Go WASH yourself SEVEN times in the JORDAN RIVER and your FLESH will be RESTORED and you will be CLEANSED."

Page 63

Elisha said, "DON'T BE AFRAID. THOSE WHO ARE WITH US ARE MORE THAN THOSE WHO ARE WITH THEM." THEN GOD OPENED THE SERVANT'S EYES AND HE SAW THE HILLS FULL OF HORSES AND CHARIOTS OF FIRE AROUND ELISHA.

Page 64

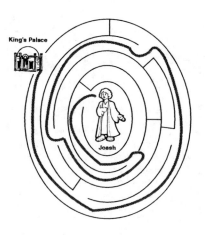

Page 65

    1. HE HELD FAST TO THE LORD AND
    2. DID NOT CEASE TO FOLLOW HIM.
    3. THE LORD MADE THE SHADOW
    4. GO BACK THE TEN STEPS IT
    5. HAD GONE DOWN ON THE STAIRWAY.

Page 66

    1. repaired   6. people
    2. temple   7. ordered
    3. read   8. people
    4. book   9. celebrate
    5. covenant   10. Passover

Page 67

WHAT HAS HAPPENED TO US IS A RESULT OF OUR EVIL DEEDS AND OUR GREAT GUILT. HERE WE ARE BEFORE YOU IN OUR GUILT, THOUGH BECAUSE OF IT NOT ONE OF US CAN STAND IN YOUR PRESENCE.

Page 68

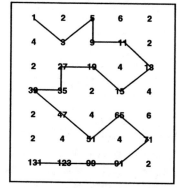

It took <u>52</u> days to rebuild the wall around Jerusalem.

Page 69

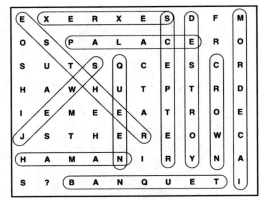

Who knows that you have come to royal position FOR SUCH A TIME AS THIS?

Page 70

I KNOW THAT MY REDEEMER LIVES, AND THAT IN THE END HE WILL STAND UPON THE EARTH. AND AFTER MY SKIN HAS BEEN DESTROYED, YET IN MY FLESH I WILL SEE GOD.

Page 71

TELL THE RIGHTEOUS IT WILL BE WELL WITH THEM, FOR THEY WILL ENJOY THE FRUIT OF THEIR DEEDS. WOE TO THE WICKED! DISASTER IS UPON THEM!

Page 72

REFORM YOU WAYS AND YOUR ACTIONS AND OBEY THE LORD YOUR GOD. THEN THE LORD WILL RELENT AND NOT BRING THE DISASTER HE HAS PRONOUNCED AGAINST YOU. AS FOR ME, I AM IN YOUR HANDS; DO WITH ME WHATEVER YOU THINK IS GOOD AND RIGHT.

Page 73

1. dry
2. skin
3. men
4. ground
5. bones
6. living
7. army
8. heard
9. sound
10. together

Ezekiel saw DRY BONES on the GROUND. Then he HEARD a rattling SOUND, and the BONES came TOGETHER. Then SKIN covered them and they became a LIVING ARMY of MEN.

Page 74

Daniel and his friends were to be trained with others to serve in the king's palace. First, Daniel's name was changed to BELTESHAZZAR, Hananiah became SHADRACH, Mishael became MESHACH, and Azariah became ABEDNEGO. When the boys being trained were given royal food and wine, Daniel and his friends chose instead to drink WATER and eat VEGETABLES. They became healthier than the others. God also blessed them and gave them KNOWLEDGE and understanding. At the end of the training period, the king questioned all the boys and found Daniel and his friends not only healthier, but TEN times smarter than even his own magicians!

Page 75

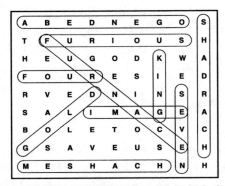

THE GOD WE SERVE IS ABLE TO SAVE US!

Page 76

THE FINGERS OF A HUMAN HAND APPEARED AND WROTE ON THE PLASTER OF THE WALL. IT WAS A MESSAGE FROM GOD THAT THE KING WAS GOING TO DIE.

Page 77

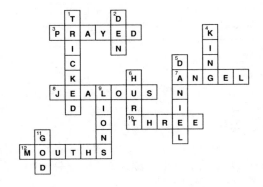

Page 78

H—preach
D—ship
F—storm
D—ship
B—sailors
C—captain

G—asleep
F—storm
A—sea
E—fish
E—fish

Page 79

MARY WILL GIVE BIRTH TO A SON, AND YOU ARE TO NAME HIM JESUS.

Page 80

1. inn
2. angels
3. manger
4. Mary
5. shepherds
6. stable
7. sheep
8. God

Joseph and MARY traveled to Bethlehem to register for the census. The INN was full, so they spent the night in a STABLE where animals were kept. Jesus was born there and his mother laid him in a MANGER to sleep. ANGELS announced His birth first to SHEPHERDS caring for their SHEEP in nearby fields. They found the baby, then praised GOD and told everyone about Jesus.

Page 81

"But you, BETHLEHEM, in the LAND of JUDAH, are by no means least among the rulers of JUDAH; for out of you will come a RULER who will be the SHEPHERD of my PEOPLE ISRAEL."
Minor Prophet: MICAH

Page 82

A: 9
B: 7
C: 4
D: 8
E: 3
F: 15
G: 19
H: 1
I: 5
J: 10
M: 18

N: 12
O: 14
P: 20
R: 11
S: 2
T: 16
V: 21
W: 6
Y: 13
Z: 17

CONFESSING THEIR SINS, THEY WERE BAPTIZED BY HIM IN THE JORDAN RIVER.

Page 83

1. WINE
2. SERVANTS
3. DISCIPLES
4. DO
5. FIRST
6. STONE
7. GLORY
8. JARS
9. MOTHER
10. CHOICE
11. MASTER
12. BANQUET
13. WATER

Page 84

1. C, POOR IN SPIRIT
2. D, MOURN
3. F, MEEK
4. B, HUNGER and THIRST for RIGHTEOUSNESS
5. G, MERCIFUL
6. E, PURE IN HEART
7. A, PEACEMAKERS
8. C, PERSECUTED BECAUSE OF RIGHTEOUSNESS

Page 85

Father, we HONOR and PRAISE your name. Let your will be done here on earth as it is done in heaven. Provide our NEEDS today. Forgive our SINS and help us to forgive people who SIN against us. Help us to RESIST temptation, and not give in to SATAN. You are our great God, all powerful, and in control of everything forever.

Page 86

WHOEVER DRINKS THE WATER I GIVE HIM WILL NEVER THIRST.

Page 87

3	7	19	5	12	9	16	23	2	11	8	4	20	21	7	3	5
17	13	99	41	6	13	24	33	22	9	44	21	109	77	99	1	9
15	11	7	43	2	32	16	9	46	7	60	66	46	9	5	43	11
19	3	11	1	6	13	4	5	14	21	23	75	18	33	19	7	9
5	103	15	9	10	7	88	93	26	5	2	12	42	73	9	3	1
53	39	77	49	97	5	17	3	91	87	51	35	5	21	1	5	5
10	2	14	33	42	4	12	19	20	67	64	20	8	15	88	75	4
12	7	1	99	26	5	18	15	76	103	25	6	59	31	36	7	8
22	44	56	47	40	6	14	1	10	79	53	80	49	3	24	12	5
80	77	3	15	9	87	82	29	4	37	91	62	55	5	36	41	10
100	53	71	9	2	73	30	39	18	29	67	12	37	29	14	15	64

Page 88

PETER'S MOTHER-IN-LAW WAS IN BED WITH A FEVER. JESUS TOUCHED HER HAND AND THE FEVER LEFT HER.
Answer to question in box: She got up and began to wait on him.

Page 89

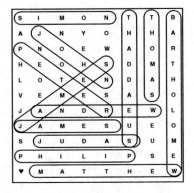

Who can be a disciple of Jesus? ANYONE WHO LOVES JESUS.

Page 90

RETURN HOME AND TELL HOW MUCH GOD HAS DONE FOR YOU.

Page 91

Page 92

1. path	5. good
2. roots	6. rocky
3. birds	7. sun
4. thorns	8. plants

A farmer planted some seeds. Some of them fell along the PATH and the BIRDS soon came and ate them. Some seeds fell on ROCKY soil.

The seeds came up but quickly died when the SUN came up because the ROOTS were too small. Some seeds fell in the soil where there were many THORNS. The seeds started to grow, but were soon crowded out by the larger THORNS. Some seeds fell on GOOD soil and grew into big, healthy PLANTS.

Page 93

HE RAN TO HIS SON, THREW HIS ARMS AROUND HIM, AND KISSED HIM.

Page 94

1. True		8. False
2. False		9. True
3. False		10. False
4. True		11. True
5. False		12. False
6. True		13. True
7. False		14. True

Page 95

2, 3

5, 1

4, 6

Page 96

1. CAME
2. THANKED
3. PRAISING
4. BACK
5. GOD
6. THREW
7. JESUS

When he saw he was healed, he CAME BACK, PRAISING GOD in a loud voice. He THREW himself at JESUS' feet and THANKED him.

Page 97

1. A		9. N
2. D		10. O
3. E		11. P
4. F		12. R
5. G		13. S
6. H		14. T
7. I		15. W
8. L		16. Y

THE GOOD SHEPHERD LAYS DOWN HIS LIFE FOR THE SHEEP.

Page 98

Jesus called in a loud voice, "Lazarus, COME OUT!" The DEAD MAN CAME OUT, his HANDS and FEET wrapped with strips of linen, and a cloth around his FACE.

Page 99

1. Zacchaeus and Jesus
2. In a tree in Jericho
3. salvation

"The SON of MAN came to SEEK and SAVE the LOST."

Page 100

Moses, Elijah

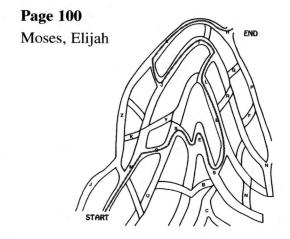

Page 101

FORGIVE OTHERS AS GOD HAS FORGIVEN YOU.

Page 102

An expert in the law asked Jesus, "WHO IS MY NEIGHBOR?"
Jesus told the story of the good Samaritan to teach this lesson: LOVE YOUR NEIGHBOR AS YOURSELF.

Page 103

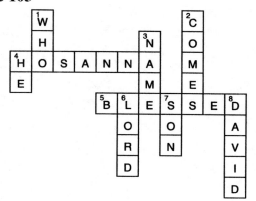

Page 104

The first servant received <u>5</u> talents, or <u>$5000</u> from his master. He doubled his money: <u>5</u> talents x <u>2</u> = <u>$10000</u>. The second servant received <u>2</u> talents, or <u>$2000</u>. He also doubled his money: <u>2</u> talents x <u>2</u> = <u>$4000</u>. The third servant received <u>1</u> talent, or <u>$1000</u>. Instead of trying to invest the money like the other servants, he buried it in a hole in a ground. <u>1</u> talent x <u>0</u> = <u>$0000</u>. He still had the <u>$1000</u> he started out with, but that was all. When the master returned, he was very pleased with the first servant who had <u>$10000</u> for him and with the second servant who had <u>$4000</u> for him. He was angry with the third servant. He took away his <u>$1000</u> and gave it to the first servant.

Page 105

PASSOVER

Page 106

MY FATHER, IF IS POSSIBLE, MAY THIS CUP BE TAKEN FROM ME. YET NOT AS I WILL, BUT AS YOU WILL.

Page 107

Peter said, "WOMAN, I DON'T KNOW HIM."
A little later someone else said, "You are one of them."
Peter replied, "MAN, I AM NOT!"
An hour later a man pointed at Peter and said, "Certainly this fellow was with him."
"MAN, I DON'T KNOW WHAT YOU'RE TALKING ABOUT!"
What did Peter do next?
HE WEPT BITTERLY.

Page 108

Jesus said, "IT IS FINISHED."
What did Jesus mean by those words? (The work of salvation was finished. His death paid for our sins.)

Page 109

1. AFRAID
2. EARTHQUAKE
3. SABBATH
4. GUARDS
5. REPORTED
6. RISEN
7. ANGEL
8. CRUCIFIED
9. TOMB
10. DISCIPLES
11. STONE
12. DAWN

Page 110

Jesus said, "You will receive POWER when the HOLY SPIRIT comes on you; and you will be my WITNESSES in JERUSALEM, and in all JUDEA and SAMARIA and to the ENDS of the EARTH."

Page 111

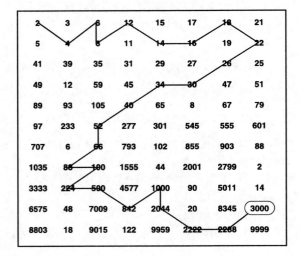

Page 112

1. APOSTLES' TEACHING and to
2. FELLOWSHIP, to the
3. BREAKING of BREAD and to
4. PRAYER
5. They met EVERY DAY.
6. They PRAISED GOD.

MY CHURCH: Students' answers will vary.

Page 113

HE WENT WITH THEM INTO THE TEMPLE COURTS, WALKING AND JUMPING, AND PRAISING GOD.

Page 114

Ananias sold a piece of PROPERTY. He gave the MONEY to the CHURCH, but kept back part of it for himself. His WIFE Sapphira knew and approved of his actions. When he laid his gift at the apostles' FEET, Peter asked him, "Why have you LIED to the HOLY SPIRIT and kept part of the MONEY for yourself? You did not have to give any of it!" Suddenly, Ananias fell down and DIED. Some men carried his body away. Later, Sapphira came in. She did not know what had happened to her HUSBAND. Peter asked her about the price Ananias had received for their PROPERTY. Sapphira also LIED. When Peter told her about Ananias' death, suddenly she fell down and DIED, too! Great FEAR filled all those who heard about Ananias and Sapphira.

Page 115

The high pri<u>est</u> said, "We gave you stri<u>ct</u> ord<u>ers</u> not to tea<u>ch</u> in this na<u>me</u>."
Peter and the others replied, "We mu<u>st</u> ob<u>ey</u> G<u>od</u> rather than m<u>en</u>!"
Bottom question: Answers will vary.

Page 116

THEY COULD NOT STAND UP AGAINST HIS WISDOM OR THE SPIRIT BY WHOM HE SPOKE.
LORD, DO NOT HOLD THIS SIN AGAINST THEM.

Page 117

1. PHILIP, ETHIOPIAN
2. In a CHARIOT on the ROAD TO GAZA
3. The man was READING. The other man told him the GOOD NEWS. The man believed and was BAPTIZED.

Page 118

4, 2
3, 6
1, 5

Page 119

BARNABAS

Page 120

MANY PEOPLE BELIEVED IN THE LORD.

Page 121

JEWS believed that GENTILES were UNCLEAN and would have nothing to do with them. CORNELIUS, whose men were on their way to ask PETER to come to his HOUSE, was a GENTILE. God wanted PETER to TEACH CORNELIUS about JESUS.

Page 122

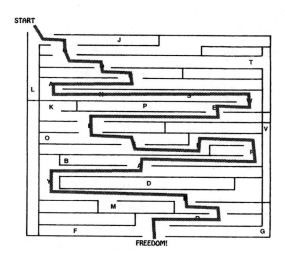

GOD ANSWERS PRAYER.

Page 123

The church in the town of ANTIOCH sent Paul and Barnabas out on this first missionary trip, and they came back there at the end of the trip.

Page 124

In Lystra, TIMOTHY joined Paul and Silas on their missionary trip.
What were the results of this second trip? The CHURCHES were strengthened in the FAITH and GREW DAILY in NUMBERS.

Page 125

In the city of Philippi Paul and Silas were beaten and then thrown into prison. The jailer put their feet in stocks to make sure they did not escape. Late that night instead of complaining, Paul and Silas were praying and singing hymns to God. The other prisoners were listening to them. Suddenly, an earthquake shook the prison! All the doors came open and everyone's chains came loose. The jailer woke up and saw the open doors. He thought all the prisoners had escaped and he was going to kill himself. Then Paul shouted to him, "We are all here!" The jailer rushed in and fell down before Paul and Silas. "What must I do to be saved?" he asked them. They told him, "Believe in the Lord Jesus and you will be saved" That night the jailer in Philippi became a Christian!

Page 126

Paul said, "I found an ALTAR inscribed to the UNKNOWN GOD. I will tell you about this God. The God who made the WORLD and EVERYTHING in it is the LORD of HEAVEN and EARTH. In Him we LIVE and MOVE and have our BEING. He will JUDGE the world with JUSTICE by the MAN He has appointed.

Answer to question: Jesus

Answer Key

Page 127

1. fell
2. ground
3. third
4. dead
5. Paul
6. himself
7. man
8. arms
9. alarmed
10. alive
11. upstairs
12. ate

Page 128

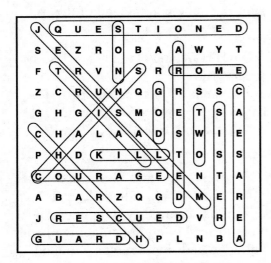

Paul went to the city of JERUSALEM. He received a warm welcome from the CHURCH, but not from some other people. An angry crowd grabbed him and tried to KILL him. Roman soldiers RESCUED him, but then ARRESTED him. They put him in CHAINS and the next day took him to be QUESTIONED by the Jewish religious leaders. That night God said to Paul, "Take COURAGE! You will testify about me in ROME." More than 40 Jews plotted to kill Paul, but the SON of his SISTER heard about it and told the Roman commander. He took Paul to CAESAREA with hundreds of soldiers to GUARD him on the way. Paul stood TRIAL before Governor Felix who then kept him around for TWO years. Finally, he was questioned by King Agrippa who said Paul should be sent to Rome, just as GOD had said!

Page 129

Paul said, "I urge you to keep up your COURAGE, because not one of you will be LOST; only the ship will be DESTROYED. Last night an ANGEL of God stood beside me and said, 'Do not be AFRAID, Paul. God has graciously given you the lives of ALL who sail with you.' I have FAITH in God that it will happen just as He told me. We will run aground on some ISLAND."

Page 130

Paul wrote about Onesimus to Philemon, "He is very dear to me but even dearer to you, both as a MAN and as a BROTHER in the Lord. WELCOME him as you would WELCOME me. If he has done you any WRONG or OWES you anything, CHARGE it to me."
Bottom question: Answers will vary.

Page 131

1. LAMB'S
2. BOOK
3. LIFE
4. LIFE
5. THRONE
6. STREETS
7. GOLD
8. ANGELS
9. GOD
10. DEATH
11. NIGHT
12. CRYING
13. SUN
14. MOON
15. TEMPLE
16. PAIN
17. LAMPS